LIGHTS, CAMERA, DUNDEE!

Thomas A. Christie and Julie Christie

Other Books by Thomas A. Christie

Liv Tyler: Star in Ascendance

The Cinema of Richard Linklater

John Hughes and Eighties Cinema: Teenage Hopes and American Dreams

Ferris Bueller's Day Off: The Pocket Movie Guide

The Christmas Movie Book

Notional Identities: Ideology, Genre and National Identity in Popular Scottish Fiction Since the Seventies

The Shadow in the Gallery

The James Bond Movies of the 1980s

Mel Brooks: Genius and Loving It!: Freedom and Liberation in the Cinema of Mel Brooks

The Spectrum of Adventure: A Brief History of Interactive Fiction on the Sinclair ZX Spectrum

A Righteously Awesome Eighties Christmas: Festive Cinema of the 1980s

Contested Mindscapes: Exploring Approaches to Dementia in Modern Popular Culture

John Hughes FAQ: All That's Left to Know About the Man Behind the Movies

The Golden Age of Christmas Movies: Festive Cinema of the 1940s and 50s

A Very Spectrum Christmas: Celebrating Seasonal Software on the Sinclair ZX Spectrum

A Totally Bodacious Nineties Christmas: Festive Cinema of the 1990s

Scotland's Christmas: Festive Celebrations, Traditions and Customs in Scotland from Samhain to Still Game
[with Murray Cook]

A Seriously Groovy Movie Christmas: Festive Cinema of the 1960s and 70s

Digital Pioneer Spirit: The Freewheeling Creative Innovation of Mel Croucher on the Home Microcomputer

Other Books by Thomas A. Christie and Julie Christie

The Heart 200 Book: A Companion Guide to Scotland's Most Exciting Road Trip

Mysteries and Secrets of the Heart 200 Route

LIGHTS, CAMERA, DUNDEE!

Filming Locations in Dundee, Tayside, and Angus

Thomas A. Christie
and Julie Christie

Lights, Camera, Dundee!: Filming Locations in Dundee, Tayside, and Angus by Thomas A. Christie and Julie Christie.

First edition published in Great Britain in 2025 by Extremis Publishing Ltd., Suite 218, Castle House, 1 Baker Street, Stirling, FK8 1AL, United Kingdom.
www.extremispublishing.com

Extremis Publishing is a Private Limited Company registered in Scotland (SC509983) whose Registered Office is Suite 218, Castle House, 1 Baker Street, Stirling, FK8 1AL, United Kingdom.

Copyright © Thomas A. Christie and Julie Christie, 2025.

Thomas A. Christie and Julie Christie have asserted the moral right under the Copyright, Designs and Patents Act 1988 to be identified as the authors of this work.

The views expressed in this work are solely those of the authors, and do not necessarily reflect those of the publisher. The publisher hereby disclaims any responsibility for them.

This book is a work of non-fiction. Unless otherwise noted, the authors and the publisher make no explicit guarantees as to the accuracy of the information included in this book and, in some cases, the names of people, places and organisations may have been altered to protect their privacy. All hyperlinks were believed to be live and correctly detailed at the time of publication.

This book may include references to organisations, feature films, television programmes, popular songs, musical bands, novels, reference books, and other creative works, the titles of which are trademarks and/or registered trademarks, and which are the intellectual properties of their respective copyright holders.

All rights reserved. No part of this publication may be reproduced, stored in a retrieval system, or transmitted, in any form or by any means, electronic, mechanical, photocopying, recording or otherwise, without the prior permission in writing of the publisher.

This book is sold subject to the condition that it shall not, by way of trade or otherwise, be lent, re-sold or hired out, or otherwise circulated without the publisher's prior consent in any form of binding or cover other than that in which it is published and without a similar condition including this condition being imposed on the subsequent purchaser.

A CIP catalogue record for this book is available from the British Library.

ISBN: 978-1-0682314-3-8

Typeset in Linux Libertine.

Printed and bound in Great Britain by IngramSpark, Chapter House, Pitfield, Kiln Farm, Milton Keynes, MK11 3LW, United Kingdom.

Cover artwork is Copyright © Jacob Boomsma at Shutterstock, all rights reserved.

Cover design and book design is Copyright © Thomas A. Christie.

Internal photographic images are sourced from the creators listed in the Image Credits section, which forms an extension to this legal page.

The copyrights of third parties are reserved. All third party imagery is used under the provision of Fair Use for the purposes of commentary and criticism. While every reasonable effort has been made to contact copyright holders and secure permission for all images reproduced in this work, we offer apologies for any instances in which this was not possible and for any inadvertent omissions.

Map of Dundee and the County of Angus

This book is dedicated to Dundee's own
Mr Eddie Small
(1951–2020)

Beloved scholar, playwright, historian,
author, encourager of writers young and old,
stalwart defender of the arts and humanities,
champion of academia,
and always the best of friends.

Contents

Introduction..Page i

1) *Dundee Courier: Production of a Great Daily Newspaper* (1911).................Page 1
2) *Bottle* (Drambuie Commercial) (1989).. Page 2
3) *Christmas in the Highlands* (2019)..Page 4
4) *Schemers* (2020)... Page 6
5) *The Silver Fleet* (1943)..Page 9
6) *An Englishman Abroad* (1983)...Page 10
7) *The Tartan Horror Story* (2009)...Page 12
8) *The Little Minister* (1975)... Page 15
9) *The Illusionist* (2011).. Page 16
10) *Dundee* (1939)...Page 19
11) *The Big Break: USA vs Europe* (2005)... Page 20
12) *Time Teens: The Beginning* (2015).. Page 22
13) *Closure* (2012)...Page 24
14) *Billy Connolly's World Tour of Scotland* (1994)..Page 27
15) *The Rubber-Keyed Wonder* (2024).. Page 28
16) *The Rise and Fall of Timex Dundee* (2019)...Page 29
17) *The New Spirit of Whisky* (2024)...Page 30
18) *The Hairy Bikers' Best of British* (2011)...Page 33
19) *Children of the City* (1944).. Page 34
20) *The Road and the Miles* (1992).. Page 35
21) *Bob Servant, Independent* (2013).. Page 37
22) *Stone of Destiny* (2008)... Page 38
23) *Go Down Swinging* (2018)... Page 40
24) *The Open Road Trip* (2022)..Page 41
25) *Christabel* (1988)...Page 42
26) *Silent Witness: In a Lonely Place* (2014)... Page 45
27) *Traces* (2019–22)...Page 46
28) *Spooked: Scotland* (2022)..Page 49
29) *Don't Let the Devil Take Another Day* (2020)..Page 50

30) *As You Like It* (1978)..Page 52
31) *Lenny Goes to Town* (1998)... Page 53
32) *The Party* (2002)...Page 54
33) *Martin Compston's Scottish Fling* (2022)..Page 57
34) *Jute City* (1991)..Page 58
35) *Brian Cox's Jute Journey* (2009).. Page 59
36) *Succession* (2019)...Page 61
37) *Billy Mackenzie: The Glamour Chase* (2000)... Page 62
38) *Christmas in the Schemes* (Music Video) (2019)..Page 64
39) *Mia* (Music Video) (2016)...Page 65
40) *Open Close Movie* (2018)... Page 66
41) *Jute, Jam and Jim McLean* (1987)... Page 69
42) *Great British Railway Journeys* (2024)...Page 70
43) *A Shot at Glory* (2000)..Page 71
44) *Under the Skin* (2013)... Page 73
45) *Moonacre* (1994)..Page 74
46) *Rat on a Highway* (2021)..Page 76
47) *1300 Shots* (2021)... Page 77
48) *The Lighthouse Stevensons* (2011)...Page 78
49) *It's My City!: Dundee, Britain's Biggest Village* (1989).............................Page 81
50) *A Life More Ordinary* (2002)..Page 82
51) *No Time* (Music Video) (2021)..Page 83
52) *Remember Us* (Music Video) (2019)..Page 85
53) *California Schemin'* (2025)..Page 86
54) *The Hidden Persuaders* (2011)... Page 88
55) *Dog Days* (2023)..Page 89
56) *Hatter's Castle* (1942)..Page 90
57) *Shopping* (Music Video) (2024)...Page 93
58) *Waterproof* (2018)... Page 94
59) *The House Was Not Hungry Then* (2025).. Page 95
60) *Frankenstein* (2025)...Page 96

Conclusion.. Page 101
Visit the Set: Locations in Dundee, Tayside and Angus...................................Page 105
Photo Credits.. Page 109
Acknowledgements... Page 113

Introduction

Dundee, Tayside, and Angus have played host to car chases and quiet heartbreaks, to epic stories and fleeting glances – moments that are captured forever by the camera lens. On screen, these streets, shorelines, and hillsides have stood in for different places all across the globe, and yet they remain unmistakably themselves. Film is memory made visible, and here in this remarkable corner of Scotland, those memories are written in light, shadow, and the ever-changing skies of the striking East Coast.

Film is more than entertainment – in a way, it is also a kind of time capsule. Every frame captures not just a story, but a particular moment in history: the fashions and faces of a specific era, the light on a certain day, the mood of a place as it once was. Long after sets have been struck and actors have moved on, the camera's gaze preserves these fleeting instants for future generations. Watching a film years later can feel like opening a window onto another world: one that seems both familiar and yet impossibly distant.

Dundee, along with the surrounding Tayside region and county of Angus, is a place that rewards such preservation. Here, the River Tay stretches out in a silver ribbon beneath skies that change by the minute, offering an inspirational, ever-shifting palette for film-makers. The city itself has always brimmed with character – a vibrant blend of historic architecture, bold modern design, and a creative spirit that has seen it rise as a UNESCO City of Design. Beyond Dundee's boundaries, Angus unfolds in a landscape of contrasts: tranquil glens, dramatic cliffs, rolling farmland, and fishing villages where centuries of tradition meet the rhythm of the tides. This is a region with a deep and revered cultural heritage, from the battles and ballads of Scotland's past to the artistic innovation of the present day.

It is little wonder, then, that so many productions – from feature films and prestige dramas to music videos and even commercials – have drawn their creative vision from here. Some have showcased these locations in all their natural glory, while others have transformed them into entirely new worlds... and yet, the true essence of the place always somehow manages to shine through. There is an authenticity in these streets, fields, and shorelines that no soundstage can ever hope to replicate.

Lights, Camera, Dundee! is a celebration of this union between place and picture. In these pages, we explore the filming locations that have brought stories to life in Dundee, Tayside, and Angus, revealing not just where these moments were captured, but why the settings resonated so meaningfully with the film-makers who chose them. Together, we'll uncover the familiar places hiding in plain sight on the silver screen, and perhaps discover new corners of the region through the eyes of the camera.

While of course it would be impossible to showcase every feature that has been filmed in this amazing part of the world, we have done our best to draw in a broad range of different films, TV features, music videos, and commercials which encompass a variety of styles and genres. Some are well-known, others perhaps more of a surprise, but all of them have made creative use of this exceptional place to bring their action to life.

In this part of Scotland, every location tells a story – and once the camera starts rolling, it becomes part of cinematic history. We hope you will enjoy this filmic odyssey around the region, and that – one day soon – you too will decide to come and visit the set for yourself.

Thomas A. Christie and Julie Christie
September 2025

LIGHTS, CAMERA, DUNDEE!

DUNDEE COURIER: PRODUCTION OF A GREAT DAILY NEWSPAPER

YEAR: 1911
DIRECTOR: George Pearson
PRODUCTION COMPANY: Gaumont

There are few staples of Dundee life that are more iconic than the long-running *Dundee Courier* newspaper, and it seems fitting that this book should start with a documentary that looked inside the production of this famed periodical – which, of course, is still going strong today. Commissioned by publishers D.C. Thomson in 1911 to commemorate half a century of the *Courier* being in print, this half-hour film is now considered a classic of early Scottish cinema.

David Couper Thomson (1861–1954), the famous founder of Dundee's D.C. Thomson & Co. Ltd. publishing company, was an enthusiastic adopter of cinema (and later television) production, and he could see the potential of these new media technologies both for business promotion and for news dissemination. *Dundee Courier: Production of a Great Daily Newspaper* was, in a real sense, a winning combination of both approaches. On one hand, it was an informative and (given its restricted length) surprisingly comprehensive guide to the high-pressure process behind producing a daily newspaper. Everything from the writing of the paper's reporters to the painstaking editing phase, all the way through to printing and distribution, was considered and depicted in the film. It offers a fascinating glimpse into the technologies of the time, including the efficiencies of using pneumatic tubes to communicate classified ads between departments, and employing the (by then well-established) linotype process for printing. Newspapers were still being transported over the River Tay by steam train to reach their geographically-widespread readership.

Thomson commissioned production company Gaumont to make the film, and it was a huge success for his business – the feature was shown widely around the Dundee area for many years, and gave audiences a rare look inside the world of journalism for which the city had rightly become so famous. Meticulously restored by the National Library of Scotland's Moving Image archive in more recent years, it remains a fascinating and informative record of a period which saw huge technological advancement.

BOTTLE (DRAMBUIE COMMERCIAL)

YEAR: 1989
DIRECTOR: Roger Woodburn
PRODUCTION COMPANY: Park Village

There can't be many evocations of Dundee Airport more memorable than that of the famous 1989 TV commercial for Drambuie Scotch whisky liqueur (a beverage originally produced by the MacKinnon family, and now by William Grant and Sons). The one minute advert was one of the most iconic of the late eighties, and was screened far and wide.

Veteran actor Robert Hardy plays the host of a formal dinner on a beautiful holiday island, but soon finds the meal under threat when he pours the last drop of Drambuie. Keen not to disappoint his guests, he promptly gets on the phone to Drambuie's Scottish headquarters, and a bottle is instantly dispatched as a top priority via a courier. The van races past the Forth Road Bridge to Dundee Airport, where the bottle then passes to a private jet. The pilot parachutes the bottle into an arid, rocky overseas environment, where another courier collects it, races off by jeep, and abseils down a cliff face to relay it to a speedboat. The boat's pilot then wastes no time in ferrying the bottle to the opulent home of the dinner host, but the estate's stuffy butler insists on presenting it to the dinner guests himself. Much to his mortification, he then trips and falls, smashing the bottle to smithereens. Bemused, the host immediately gets back on the phone to Drambuie again.

Bottle was a striking evocation of a Scotland which was simultaneously at the cutting edge of business and yet comfortably traditional, and with its distinctive imagery the advert became a standard-bearer for 'Scotland the Brand.' Acclaimed piper Martyn Bennett played a reel on the smallpipes to accompany the frenetic action. The appearance of Dundee Airport may be brief, but it emphasised the importance of Tayside as a commercial hub with links not only around Scotland and the UK, but to the wider world too. A sequel to the commercial was later produced (along very similar lines) in the late nineties, with famed actor Robert Powell now taking centre stage as the beleaguered dinner host. This time, a more *James Bond*-themed journey takes place with skiers, speedboats, and fast cars in Mediterranean settings, and – in spite of the abandonment of the earlier advert's Scottish settings – Robert Hardy still enjoyed a brief cameo with a playful wink to camera.

CHRISTMAS IN THE HIGHLANDS

YEAR: 2019
DIRECTOR: Ryan Dewar
PRODUCTION COMPANY: Triventure Films

Christmas-themed TV movies have become an enduringly popular part of the festive season in recent years, and Scotland has not been forgotten as a culturally rich setting for these cosily inviting Yuletide romances. Ryan Dewar's *Christmas in the Highlands* saw the East Coast take centre stage, as the film made the most of some arresting locations throughout Angus and Highland Perthshire as it depicted a Christmas adventure that was, simultaneously, highly traditional and yet strangely unconventional.

The story involves New York City perfume sales manager Blair (Brooke Burfitt), who is dispatched by her pushy, hard-headed boss Mrs Ferdi (Caprice Bourret) to the Highlands of Scotland in order to negotiate for the rights to reproduce a rare perfume belonging to the family of the Duke of Glenmorie (a wryly well-observed supporting performance by veteran actor Nicholas Farrell). So desperate is this entrepreneurial martinet to acquire such a distinctive product, she thinks nothing of sending her young employee abroad at the height of the Christmas holidays – and with the stern warning that if she is unable to succeed, her job is in the balance. Little does Blair realise that this uphill struggle will become considerably more complicated when she meets the Duke's charming son, Alistair (Dan Jeanotte), who is immediately smitten by the beautiful American visitor. Their budding relationship is complicated by some familial chicanery engineered by the devious Lady McLeod (Geraldine Somerville) and Alistair's scheming brother Robert (Olly Bassi), leading to a dramatic showdown at the aristocratic family's annual festive ball. But can the plotting of these blue-blooded backstabbers be thwarted in time for true love to prevail?

This film has been a regularly-screened modern exponent of Christmas cinema and TV movies that would use Scotland as the backdrop for their festive action. Others have included *A Christmas Carol* (David Izatt, 2018); *Lost at Christmas* (Ryan Hendrick, 2020); *A Castle for Christmas* (Mary Lambert, 2021); *Saving Christmas Spirit* (Wendy Faraone, 2022); *Christmas in Scotland* (David Lumsden, 2023); *A Merry Scottish Christmas* (Dustin Rikert,

2023); and *A Scottish Christmas Secret* (Graham Pritz-Bennett, 2025). While there were stalwart performances from Nicholas Farrell as the benignly endearing Duke, and Geraldine Somerville relishing the villainous machinations of the Machiavellian Lady McLeod, Caprice Bourret comes close to stealing the show with her over-the-top portrayal of the demanding, entitled Mrs Ferdi – a New York business mogul who is singularly unused to hearing the word 'no.' That being said, eyebrows were raised amongst some reviewers who found the casting of the central couple to be vaguely puzzling. The dashing Alistair is played by Montreal-born Canadian actor Dan Jeanotte, whose evocation of an impeccable Oxford RP accent suggests more about the character's elite education than his authentic Scottish roots. Yet to play the New York-based Blair, English/New Zealand actor and radio presenter Brooke Burfitt was chosen, and portrays the character with a creditable metropolitan East Coast American accent in spite of her own natural inflection being more closely aligned with the Home Counties of England. Similarly, some of the film's plot twists were so contrived that they stretched credulity to breaking point – including a wild deer which has an inexplicable penchant for stealing designer handbags. But unlikely situations aside, in the grand tradition of appealing Christmas romances the blossoming love of our heroes somehow manages to overcome even the least plausible of situations in order to flourish.

With an atmospheric original score by Ian Fisher and some beautifully-judged cinematography from Miroslaw Czubszek, *Christmas in the Highlands* (which was entitled *Christmas at the Castle* for the North American market) makes use of some truly eye-catching locations in the counties of Angus and Perthshire including Pitlochry, Grandtully, and most especially stately Glamis Castle which is used to depict the fictional home of the Duke of Glenmorie. Glamis was the childhood residence of Queen Elizabeth, The Queen Mother, and the late Princess Margaret was born there in 1930. The castle is a Category A listed building, and is now the home of the Earl of Strathmore and Kinghorne. Certain parts of the building are open to the public during the year, and guided tours may include some of the well-known areas which are depicted in the film. Other locations used throughout this TV movie include the Edinburgh Christmas Market, the Tayside Christmas Tree Farm, and the grand ballroom of the Royal College of Physicians in Edinburgh. The fictional perfumery belonging to the Duke's family was filmed at Castle Forbes, near Alford in Aberdeenshire, where the Forbes family has been creating the finest quality of fragrances and candles since 1996.

SCHEMERS

YEAR: 2020
DIRECTOR: Dave McLean
PRODUCTION COMPANY: Black Factory Films/Riverman Scotland/Schemers Film

Filmed and set entirely in Dundee, *Schemers* was an urban crime drama with a darkly comic edge. Written by Dave McLean, Kyle Titterton, and Khaled Spiewak, the film loosely took its inspiration from McLean's formative years living in the city prior to him becoming the manager of alternative rock band Placebo. *Schemers* won the Audience Award at the Edinburgh International Award Festival, and was also nominated for a Raindance Award at the Raindance Film Festival.

The action of *Schemers* was set in 1979, and follows the misadventures of the hapless Davie (Conor Berry). A footballer from Dundee's council schemes, Davie is an inveterate hustler with a monumentally bad run of luck at gambling. When an injury ends his hopes of a long-term football career, he finds himself at a loose end, but soon becomes deeply attracted to a student nurse named Shona (Tara Lee) and decides to impress her by setting up a disco. Davie and his friends John (Grant Robert Keelan) and Scot (Sean Connor) are soon promoting increasingly successful bands, but this inadvertently causes them to go into debt with notorious gangster Fergie (Alastair Thomson Mills) – a very bad place to be. In order to win Shona's heart, avoid Fergie's retribution, and establish his reputation while paying off his liabilities, Davie must somehow arrange a gig for the legendary band Iron Maiden at Dundee's famous Caird Hall. There's only one problem: how can he possibly pull it off?

As well as scenes at the Caird Hall itself (where Iron Maiden did indeed perform in concert at the Caird Hall on 12th June 1980), *Schemers* featured many well-known Dundee locations, not least the legendary Groucho's record shop. Originally opened in Perth Road in 1976 (when it was known as Breeks), Groucho's is now situated on the Nethergate at the epicentre of Dundee's student life, and has been beloved by generations of Dundonian music lovers. It is currently a music bar. The Beat Generator Live music venue also made an appearance in the film. Based in the city's North Lindsay Street, it is universally recognised as a titan of Scotland's independent music scene.

THE SILVER FLEET

YEAR: 1943
DIRECTORS: Vernon Sewell and Gordon Wellesley
PRODUCTION COMPANY: The Archers/The Royal Navy/The Royal Netherland Government

The Silver Fleet was a British war drama produced during World War II by the famous production duo Michael Powell and Emeric Pressburger. Designed to encourage hope and positivity at one of the darkest times in history – as was the case for so many films of the time – it featured many well-known British acting talents of the time such as Ralph Richardson, Googie Withers, Esmond Knight, and Valentine Dyall.

The film concerns Dutch submarine shipyard operator Jaap van Leyden (Ralph Richardson), a skilled engineer who is coerced into collaboration with the occupying Nazis when they invade the Netherlands. In reality, he becomes convinced of the need to fight for freedom and becomes a saboteur, culminating in an internecine plot where twelve Dutch engineers hijack a brand new U-boat and steer it – along with its incarcerated Nazi crew – to Britain for capture. Van Leyden's schemes grow ever more audacious, and after a second submarine is constructed at the shipyard he plans to encourage a party of senior Nazi officers to accompany him on its maiden voyage and then detonate a bomb in the engine room. This will not only assassinate the enemy occupiers but will also deprive Hitler's regime of another U-boat. However, the Dutch resistance – not suspecting van Leyden's involvement in opposing the Nazi occupation – ironically seem fated to disrupt the plan at the last minute. Can the courageous engineer succeed against the odds?

Given the time of production during the Second World War, locations available to the filmmakers were limited. Much of *The Silver Fleet* was filmed in and around venues and places based in Cheshire and Norfolk, using civic buildings in King's Lynn and dockland settings near the village of Port Sunlight on the Wirral as well as Birkenhead. However, the film was not without its Scottish influences, as the Eastern Wharf in the Port of Dundee was used as the berth for the fictional U-boat, *U108*, with the pier of the Fish Dock visible in the distance. *The Silver Fleet* proved popular with audiences, and won two Photoplay Awards (for Best Picture and Best Performance for Ralph Richardson) in August 1945.

AN ENGLISHMAN ABROAD

YEAR: 1983
DIRECTOR: John Schlesinger
PRODUCTION COMPANY: British Broadcasting Corporation

Few productions have made such inventive use of Dundee's city centre than *An Englishman Abroad*, the famous BBC TV movie from the pen of acclaimed playwright Alan Bennett, which took place in Moscow at the height of the Cold War. The feature concerns the tour of the Shakespeare Memorial Theatre – the first visit of a major British theatre company to the Soviet Union – between December 1958 and January 1959. There, actor Coral Browne, who was playing the character of Gertrude in the company's production of *Hamlet*, unexpectedly encounters Guy Burgess – the notorious Cambridge University-educated double agent. The feature was based on a real-life encounter between the pair, albeit somewhat embellished for dramatic effect. In a fascinating twist, Browne portrayed her 45-year-old self in the film in spite of nearing the age of 70 in real life, while Burgess was played by Alan Bates.

The film's action is deliberately low-key, with emphasis very much on character and dialogue. During a December staging of *Hamlet* in Moscow of 1958, actor Coral Browne is startled when she is visited unexpectedly in her dressing room by none other than Guy Burgess: a British agent who had defected to the Soviet Union seven years earlier, when he had discovered that he was under investigation by his own side due to his communist leanings. Though he is inebriated when they meet, she finds him an engaging and cultured character; he doesn't identify himself, but another actor from the troupe recognises him and explains who Browne's mysterious visitor had been. Through a note the next day, Burgess invites Browne for lunch at his apartment in Moscow (which proves to be something of a challenge to track down, given her lack of familiarity with the city), and they engage in conversation. Browne discovers that he is despondent about his fate, if unrepentant for his earlier actions. It transpires that he wants her to take his measurements for a new suit that he would like tailored in London. She is somewhat surprised by his request, but does as he asks and – upon her return to England – takes the notes to a series of expensive firms in London as she seeks to meet his exacting requirements.

Though some scenes were actually filmed in Inverness, it is for its Dundee location filming that *An Englishman Abroad* has become most fondly-remembered. While Dundee High School, the Whitehall Theatre, and the Clydesdale Bank all appear as Muscovite venues, perhaps the defining sequence of the film takes place at the Caird Hall – expertly transformed into the exterior of the a theatre in the heart of Moscow. Giant banners of Karl Marx, Friedrich Engels, and Vladimir Lenin were hung amongst the Hall's Doric columns, their faces dominating the City Square. While there had been plenty of snow in Scotland during the time of filming, it had somehow managed to bypass Dundee entirely, leading to some dramatic licence from the production crew – in order to replicate wintry Moscow, sixty tonnes of salt were distributed by Tayside Regional Council around the filming area to stand in for drifting snowfall. Ironically, while the Council scrupulously removed all of the salt from the area overnight so that it didn't affect pedestrian traffic the following morning, a real blizzard took place just a few days afterwards.

The production crew also redressed some shops in the Dundee city centre, replacing signage with temporary frontages showing Cyrillic Russian lettering and placing period-appropriate goods in the windows – all to keep up the accurate facade of the oppressive Soviet Moscow environment. Additionally, the film used Glasgow City Chambers (and its famous marble staircase) to portray the British Embassy, as well as the St Andrew's Suspension Bridge in Glasgow, while the exterior of Burgess's flat was filmed at Moss Heights in Cardonald. Fortunately for the filmmakers, there was heavy snowfall in Glasgow at the time of filming, which tended to obscure any obvious visual inaccuracies.

While John Schlesinger's direction was widely praised by critics, there were many other noteworthy aspects to the production, from George Fenton's contemplative original score to the many solid supporting performances by Charles Gray, Vernon Dobtcheff, Harold Innocent, and Mark Wing-Davey as the Shakespearean actors bringing *Hamlet* to life for Cold War Muscovites. *An Englishman Abroad* won a staggering nine BAFTA TV Awards, as well as a Royal Television Society Award for Alan Bates, and even today stands as a highlight of Alan Bennett's storied writing career. The play was later adapted by Bennett for BBC World Service radio in 1994 – with Michael Gambon as Guy Burgess and Penelope Wilton portraying Coral Browne (the real Browne having passed away a few years earlier in 1991) – to considerable acclaim from commentators.

THE TARTAN HORROR STORY

YEAR: 2009
DIRECTORS: Sandy Jack and Stephen Samson
PRODUCTION COMPANY: Never Lost Productions

Not every film to be shot in the Tayside and Angus areas can claim to be a Hollywood blockbuster. *The Tartan Horror Story* was a micro-budget production, with an estimated budget in the region of £1,000, and yet it uses its resources very judiciously to produce an atmospheric feature which brims with local character.

This unconventional slasher horror featured its directors Sandy Jack and Stephen Samson in the lead roles, along with actors Mhairi White and Ami Woodford. Like many independent films, the feature had a long gestation period, initially being shot around the year 2002 with an intended 2003 release date. However, it didn't actually reach the point of commercial release until some years later, in 2009.

The film aims to generate horror through the lens of the familiar, juxtaposing the well-known sights of Dundee with the visceral suspense for which the thriller genre has become so widely known. A young woman sets out to find her missing sister, little knowing that her search will become increasingly desperate – and perilous – as her investigations continue. Many of the techniques used to great effect in modern horror features were present and correct, from jump scares and a growing sense of foreboding through to a homage to the 'found footage' approach which had been popularised by films such as *The Blair Witch Project* (Daniel Myrick and Eduardo Sánchez, 1999) and others.

The Tartan Horror Story features many locations in and around urban Dundee, not least the High Street and Murraygate, along with a number of nearby industrial venues. The beach at the nearby Tayside town of Monifieth is also memorably used in coastal scenes, which appear as a welcome contrast to the often-claustrophobic action that makes up a majority of the film. The directors certainly had an uphill struggle in getting the feature onto screens: a camera bag full of equipment was stolen at one point during the production, leaving the filmmakers with no option but to resort to reshoots of the substantial amount of footage that had been lost in the theft.

THE LITTLE MINISTER

YEAR: 1975
DIRECTOR: Cedric Messina
PRODUCTION COMPANY: British Broadcasting Corporation

In November 1975, the BBC's *Play of the Month* was a TV version of J.M. Barrie's novel *The Little Minister* (1891), which was originally adapted for stage back in 1897. The story had reached the big screen in 1915 as a silent British movie, before being remade as American productions in 1921, 1922, and 1934, so an updating of the Victorian-era tale was long overdue at the time it was filmed. The BBC adaptation was a celebrated, star-studded feature, where stars Helen Mirren and Ian Ogilvy were supported by a plethora of celebrated character actors including Peter Barkworth, Nicholas Jones, and David Bailie.

The Rev. Gavin Dishart (Ian Ogilvy) is appointed minister of a church in the rural Scottish village of Thrums. The community is in the throes of major changes as a result of the Industrial Revolution, with old traditions being swept away; a labour riot has recently taken place, and military retribution seems inevitable. Dishart meets the enigmatic Babbie (Helen Mirren), an independently-minded young woman who stirs up discord against the approaching soldiers. Because his faith makes him more inclined towards diplomacy than resistance, they are immediately at odds, and yet find themselves (though they might deny it) increasingly attracted to each other. However, Babbie is considerably more than she seems, and Dishart must come to terms with the fact that to marry her would be in contravention of his religious beliefs – to say nothing of risking the ire of his congregation.

Just as had been the case with Barrie's novel, *The Little Minister* explored the juxtaposition between love and duty, the conflict between religious hypocrisy and the responsibilities of faith, and the way that the socio-economic tensions of the period impacted on social conventions and modes of industry. Though the action is centred on the fictional settlement of 'Thrums' – a weaving village thought to be loosely based on Barrie's real-life Angus home town of Kirriemuir – filming took place principally in and around the grand estate of Glamis Castle, making the most of this remarkable building. Director Cedric Messina was so enthused by the visual grandeur and atmosphere of the castle, it inspired him to produce an ambitious series of televised Shakespearean plays soon afterwards.

THE ILLUSIONIST

YEAR: 2010
DIRECTOR: Sylvain Chomet
PRODUCTION COMPANY: Pathé/Django Films/Allied Filmmakers

While live action features may dominate in discussions about Dundee's contribution to TV and film, it's important to remember that animated works are just as significant to its success. The French language film *The Illusionist* (*l'Illusionniste*) was a highly distinctive collaboration between creative teams in France and Scotland, bringing to life the work of one of France's most beloved heroes of cinematic comedy.

The genesis of *The Illusionist* can be traced back to a screenplay written by the French director, actor, and mime Jacques Tati back in 1956. The script was developed but ultimately never produced, and there was much controversy over the fact that Tati is thought to have intended the work as an appeal for personal rapprochement between himself and his long-estranged daughter, Helga Marie-Jeanne Schiel. Decades later, director Sylvain Chomet mounted an ambitious creative attempt to bring Tati's unproduced work to life, but whereas Tati had initially intended the screenplay to be the basis of a live action film, it was instead decided to develop it into an animated feature instead. Chomet, who had won international acclaim for his earlier animated film *The Triplets of Belleville* (2003), established an animation studio named Django Films in Edinburgh in 2004, and this may have been one of the reasons for his creative decision to relocate the action of *The Illusionist* from post-War Prague (in then-Czechoslovakia) to late-1950s Scotland. The central character bears a strong resemblance, both visually and in terms of quirks and mannerisms, to an elderly version of the late Tati himself.

The plot of the film focuses on the travails of an illusionist who, unsure of his place in a world of new and exciting entertainments, finds himself feeling listless and archaic. Disenchanted, he decides to leave his native Paris in search of new opportunities, and eventually winds up in London – where he similarly feels like an obsolete relic of a bygone age. However, a chance encounter with an inebriated partygoer leads him to an invitation to an island off the coast of Scotland, where he soon finds himself in his element keeping the residents enraptured by his tricks. There, he encounters a young girl named Alice who comes to believe that the illusionist is not a stage magician but rather a wizard with real supernatural powers. She follows him to Edinburgh, where he plays to minuscule audiences at a run-down theatre. Alice is happy there, and soon becomes a surrogate daughter to the old man, but she is unaware that his straitened financial circumstances have led him to trade his illusionist's equipment at a pawn shop and instead seek employment in increasingly humbling roles that use none of his extensive stage skills. Eventually Alice finds love, and the illusionist realises that his unofficial paternal role is at an end. Leaving her a gift of what little money he has left, he releases his stage rabbit on Arthur's Seat in a symbolic gesture (where it quickly encounters new friends), and boards a train headed for an unknown destination. In a final act of sleight-of-hand talent, the illusionist performs one last trick to the delight of an infant who is a fellow passenger on the train.

While *The Illusionist* is set predominantly in Edinburgh, it still retains a creative connection to Dundee as a result of the involvement of ink.digital, an animation studio based in the city which joined forces with Django Films to work on the feature. Along with other production companies, including in Paris (the Neomis Animation Studio) and South Korea, the film was a true international co-operation which was estimated to have cost around £8.5 million, funded by Pathé Pictures. Estimates of the entire personnel involved in the production of the film have ranged from 180 to 300 creatives (depending on which source is consulted), including around 80 animators.

The Illusionist met with rapturous acclaim from critics, and was nominated for a Golden Globe Award, Academy Award, and Annie Award. It would go on to win Best Animated Feature Film at the European Film Awards, and the César Award for Best Animated Feature. There was particular praise for stars Jean-Claude Donda and Eilidh Rankin. For all its melancholic sentiment, the film contained a number of judicious in-jokes which were sure to delight long-time Tati fans, including the appearance of the director's famous film *Mon Oncle* (1958) at The Cameo theatre, while at one point – while attempting to hide – the illusionist is disguised as Tati's celebrated comic creation, Monsieur Hulot. The pawnbrokers visited by the illusionist was based on the exterior of the Duncanson and Edwards shop in Edinburgh, and there was also a brief appearance by the policeman character from Chomet's 1996 feature *The Old Lady and the Pigeons* (*La vielle dame et les pigeons*), who can be seen when the illusionist is boarding the boat which is heading for the unnamed island located off the Scottish coast.

DUNDEE

YEAR: 1939
DIRECTOR: Donald Alexander
PRODUCTION COMPANY: Scottish Films Productions

Dundee, a short documentary film from the 1930s, has proven to be a fascinating snapshot of life in the city during the inter-war period. Focusing on the social, technological, and industrial changes that were driving the development of Tayside at the time, it was a relentlessly optimistic and thoroughly modern evocation of Dundee which still didn't shy away from some of the more difficult events that had faced the community over the years.

Thought to have been filmed in 1937, *Dundee* was scheduled to be screened in the city at a meeting of the British Association, which was set to take place on the 3rd of September 1939. However, due to Prime Minister Neville Chamberlain's declaration of war against Germany on that same date, the screening was halted during the screening, and – with the horrors of World War II just around the corner – it was ultimately never to be commercially released. *Dundee* would be the last feature that was to be sponsored by the inaugural Films of Scotland Committee before it was discontinued on account of the demands of wartime. The feature now resides in the Scottish Film Archive Collection.

Donald Alexander's film, which was narrated by Alastair Borthwick and Tom Smith, delivers a fascinating overview of Dundee life through various interviews with Dundonians of different ages and backgrounds. There is particular emphasis on the establishment of the jute industry in the early nineteenth century and an exploration of why this material, often used to create inexpensive cloth, was so vitally central to the city's prosperity during this period.

Graham Thomson's photography makes great use of the River Tay as a canvas for the unfolding feature, emphasising the importance of the Rail Bridge for transporting raw materials into Dundee and then delivering products out to the wider world. The depiction is of a vibrant and bustling city, and it is poignant to reflect that the film-makers and interviewees would of course have been completely unaware of the damage that would be inflicted by German Luftwaffe bombing raids in the months and years following the documentary's production.

THE BIG BREAK: USA vs EUROPE

YEAR: 2005
DIRECTORS: Various Directors
PRODUCTION COMPANY: The Golf Channel

Not to be confused with the BBC's long-running, similarly-titled snooker quiz (1990–2002), The Golf Channel's *The Big Break* was a popular reality TV show which ran from 2003 to 2015. Every year, would-be professional golfers were invited to compete on some of the world's most celebrated golf courses, with the ultimate prize being exemptions into selected golf events or even full-season exemptions on specific golfing tours. The first three seasons of the show had focused on golf courses in Michigan, Nevada, and Virginia in the United States, but for their fourth season in 2005 a different destination was in the sights of the production crew: the world-famous Carnoustie Golf Course.

Presented by Vince Cellini and Stephanie Sparks, the show loosely followed the format of the Ryder Cup by pitching golfers from America and Europe against each other. Competitors from the USA were drawn from the States of California, Florida, Texas, South Carolina, Michigan, and Massachusetts, while the European players were based in England, France, Switzerland, and the Netherlands. Filmed in the June of 2005 (and broadcast in the September of that year), the action was split over two locations: Carnoustie Golf Links and the similarly-renowned Old Course at St Andrews. The top prizes included exemptions into two significant golfing events – the Celtic Manor Wales Open and the Algarve Open de Portugal – as well as an endorsement deal with sports equipment company Bridgestone Golf Inc.

This run of the show featured a number of distinctive competitors, including British golfer Marty Wilde Jr. (son of singer Marty Wilde and brother of Kim Wilde) and American T.J. Valentine (son of professional bowler Jeffrey Valentine). The eventual winner of the hotly-contested competition was Paul Holtby of Simi Valley, California. As might be expected, the beautiful and meticulously-maintained golf course at Carnoustie has rarely looked quite so appealing as it does here, and the show made abundantly clear why it is considered not only internationally renowned, but also so challenging even for the most talented golfer.

TIME TEENS: THE BEGINNING

YEAR: 2015
DIRECTOR: Ryan Alexander Dewar
PRODUCTION COMPANY: Baudelaire Productions/Dreamcastle Films/Theatre Arts School

Time Teens: The Beginning is a remarkably ambitious science fiction feature written by Ian Grieve, a Scottish actor/director who encountered filmmaker Ryan Dewar during Grieve's tenure as a resident director at Perth Theatre and agreed to collaborate on the project. *Time Teens: The Beginning* was based on a series of Grieve's unproduced TV scripts, written around a decade beforehand, and acted as a prequel to the action of the mooted television series. In spite of its speculative fiction premise, the action was very much based in Scotland and drew upon an impressive cast of actors (many of whom were local to the Perth area, where most of the action is situated).

William (Ian Grieve) is a time traveller (or 'Tourasaiche') who is tasked by the World Time Forum with maintaining law and order across the timelines. He is situated in Perth, under the authority of the Council of Nine. However, everything changes when he receives a mysterious letter which was written in the future, warning him of dire consequences if he maintains his present trajectory. Shaken, he resolves to change his fate by assembling a team that has the ability to alter the future before it even happens. But is everything quite as it seems, or is William's situation even more complicated than it first appears?

This inexpensive independent feature (with a production budget estimated at £5,000) was something of a *tour de force* for the production team; in spite of running for a duration of nearly two hours, all of the filming took place within a total of sixteen days between 2013 and 2014, with the editing process lasting for barely two months – a remarkable achievement. While it is mostly situated within the Perth area, the time-jumping plot sees the action shift between different eras including the Victorian period and a rather dystopian technocratic future. Due to its setting, the production achieved significant attention in Perth, with local businesses enthusiastically getting behind it (both in terms of sponsorship and in-kind support) in order to ensure that it achieved release. Perhaps most astonishingly of all, altruistic actors – both new and established – waived their fees in order to see the project come to life, which proved to be an essential aspect in getting it off the ground.

For all its micro-budget challenges, the film boasted an extensive cast led by Grieve himself along with Andy Gray, who had appeared in many stage and television roles ranging from *Rab C. Nesbitt* to *Two Thousand Acres of Sky*, but remained – for many – forever best-known as the affable Glasgow con-man Charles 'Chancer' Chalmers in the BBC's celebrated sitcom *City Lights*. Other prominent members of the cast included Liam Brennan, Ralph Riach, Tom McGovern, and Annie Louise Ross.

The film was exhibited all across Scotland following its premiere at the Perth Playhouse Cinema, with screenings in Aberdeenshire and Fife. The creative accomplishment of the filmmakers was recognised at the San Francisco Film Awards 2025, where Ryan Dewar was presented with the International Film Award of Excellence. It also won awards at the San Francisco Film Awards and International Independent Film Awards, as well as nominations at the International Euro Film Festival and the Deep Fried Film Festival.

Time Teens: The Beginning was filmed in a number of locations around Perth including Perth Museum and the Zoo Nightclub, as well as – most relevant to this book – the Lowson Memorial Church in Forfar, Angus, and the grand exterior of Glamis Castle. Built in 1914, the Lowson Memorial Church was constructed in the Scots Gothic style by architect Alexander Marshall MacKenzie, and is one of the most prominent Church of Scotland buildings in Forfar (located just off Montrose Road). The Category A listed church, with its distinctive spire and Douglas Strachan-produced stained glass, was exactly the kind of atmospheric locale that the film could make full use of – not least given that its traditional appearance was an effective contrast with the futuristic locales elsewhere in the action.

With its impressive aspirations, it won't seem too surprising to learn that *Time Teens: The Beginning* was intended as a kind of 'backdoor pilot' for a subsequent television series, with the action culminating in a conclusion that suggested the general direction that a TV continuation might take. As of the time of writing, no such spin-off has come to fruition, but – as it stands – the film is a noteworthy example of what can be achieved with filmmaking talent, writing and performance skill, and the unstinting support of the local community, even on the most modest of budgets.

CLOSURE

YEAR: 2012
DIRECTORS: Andrew Golden and Joel Hewitt
PRODUCTION COMPANY: Finger Clock

With its varied architecture and boundless personality, Dundee is the perfect location for features which explore its urban landscape, and the city has lent itself well to character-based dramas over the years. One of them was *Closure*, a feature in the 'mumblecore' mode which focused on the main characteristics of that subgenre of film: low budget, action stressing the significance of dialogue over plot, concentrating on the relationships between adults, filming in real places rather than sound stages or studio sets, and maintaining a naturalistic performance style throughout.

The film centres on the relationship between two people, Daniel (Joel Hewitt) and Eve (Sarah Calmus), with a vital twist — it follows their romance by starting at its emotional conclusion and then working backwards to their first meeting. In reverse, we see the love affair between them as it develops, weakens, and eventually falls apart. Daniel is a walking contradiction, simultaneously keen to succeed and yet unable to resist slacking; on one hand, he is practical and ambitious, and on the other he is a fun-loving student keen to embrace the last fun-filled years of youth before a lifetime of adult responsibilities kick in. One night, at a party, he meets Eve and is immediately attracted to the fact that she seems to embody everything he doesn't. Opposites attract, and the two find themselves drawn together... only to discover that sometimes people who seem wildly dissimilar may actually be too alike.

With location filming in Dundee and Tayport, *Closure* was produced in black and white on a tiny budget in the region of £150, but it makes the most of cast of unknowns – mostly drawn from the local area – to produce a plethora of memorable characters. (The film's co-director, Andrew Golden, appears in a cameo appearance as a party guest.) It proved popular on Tayside, with the first two screenings of the film being sold out completely within less than an hour. As *Closure*'s tagline explains, it is a feature about beginnings and endings – and in practice, it demonstrates that the two don't necessarily need to unfold in a strictly linear order.

BILLY CONNOLLY'S WORLD TOUR OF SCOTLAND

YEAR: 1994
DIRECTOR: Willy Smax
PRODUCTION COMPANY: British Broadcasting Corporation

In early 1994, stand-up comedian Billy Connolly – who had achieved immense international fame at this point in his career – decided to get back to his roots and take part in a 54-date performance tour of his native Scotland. Kicking off the tour in Greenock, he visited cities, towns, and villages across the country, and this six-part documentary series (a creative collaboration between Connolly, Steve Brown, and Nobby Clark) followed him as he discusses places of cultural and historic importance as well as those which had established a particular connection with him on a personal level.

The fifth episode of the series, broadcast on the 9th of August 1994, brought Connolly to Angus and Dundee, where he tasted some world-renowned Arbroath Smokies before making his way to Dundee Law – the remains of a volcanic sill overlooking the city which is the highest and most prominent point on the Dundee skyline. At the crest of the Law is a War Memorial, and Connolly chose this location to recite William McGonagall's infamous poem *The Tay Bridge Disaster* (1880) in sight of the (new) Tay Rail Bridge in the far distance.

Commemorating the tragic collapse of the original Tay Bridge in December 1879, when 75 people lost their lives (not 90, as McGonagall erroneously chronicles it), *The Tay Bridge Disaster* is widely considered to be one of the worst poems in Scottish history, and cemented McGonagall's reputation for rambling detail, repetitiveness, a sledgehammer approach to poetic metaphor, and implausible rhyme schemes. As Connolly circles the Dundee War Memorial while he gleefully recites the notoriously bad verse (thus popularising McGonagall's unwitting comic charm for a whole new generation), an unexpected blizzard took place, with an estimated two inches of snow falling on Dundee as the sequence unfolds. Undeterred, his battered anthology of McGonagall's work all but illegible as the fresh snow battered down, Connolly gamely persevered until he reached the poem's conclusion.

The series was a huge success with viewers, and the format paved the way for many future travelogues featuring Connolly, covering locations from North America to Australasia.

THE RUBBER-KEYED WONDER

YEAR: 2024
DIRECTORS: Anthony Caulfield and Nicola Caulfield
PRODUCTION COMPANY: Gracious Films/PlayerUnknown Productions

Dundee is a city often associated with computer technology, even from the earliest days of home microcomputing in the 1980s. While it has hosted many innovative games design companies in recent decades, and its digital economy continues to thrive today, one of its greatest claims to fame was the famous Dundee Timex factory which was situated on the city's Harrison Road. It was this factory whose large, highly-skilled workforce was responsible for manufacturing the Sinclair ZX Spectrum microcomputer in the early 1980s, thus kick-starting the modern British computing revolution; from kids discovering computer games for the first time through to the boom in 'bedroom coding' (where people could code and distribute software titles on cassette tape – all from the comfort of their spare room), the Timex factory's legacy to computing continues to loom large even today.

The husband-and-wife documentary film-making team of Anthony and Nicola Caulfield had achieved considerable success amongst retro gaming enthusiast thanks to their feature *From Bedrooms to Billions* (2014) – which focused on the independent game design revolution of the 1980s – and its various sequels, and *The Rubber-Keyed Wonder* continued to demonstrate their reputation for factual accuracy and historical reflection. The documentary follows Sir Clive Sinclair's determination to make computer technology affordable and accessible to everyone, and the Timex factory proved to be a natural partner in this goal; having had years of experience in manufacturing digital watches, switching over to the circuit boards of home microcomputers seemed like an inescapable progression.

Today, the Sinclair ZX Spectrum continues to be fondly remembered by an entire generation, and – at the height of the machine's fame – the Timex factory was manufacturing a new unit every four seconds in order to meet demand. It was to be a major factor in the establishment of Dundee's video game industry, linking the city to the emergent global technological industry and boosting the local economy. *The Rubber-Keyed Wonder* had its Scottish premiere at the Dundee Contemporary Arts Centre on the 24th of November 2024, and featured a Q&A session with directors Nicola and Anthony Caulfield.

THE RISE AND FALL OF TIMEX DUNDEE

YEAR: 2019
DIRECTOR: Andy Twaddle
PRODUCTION COMPANY: British Broadcasting Corporation

The Timex factory was a significant player in Dundee's economy, first opening in 1947 as a centre for mechanical wristwatch production. At the peak of its success during the digital watch boom, the factory employed between 6,000 and 7,000 staff, though this had dwindled to 4,200 by the early 1980s as the manufacturing emphasis shifted to electronics such as the aforementioned Sinclair ZX Spectrum microcomputer and the contract for the famous Nimslo 3D camera (a lenticular camera which could produce 3D images that didn't require glasses to view) came to an end. The workforce, 80% of which was composed of women, was both highly capable and very versatile, moving effortlessly from the manufacturing of one complex product to another.

By 1992, however, the workforce at the Timex factory had been reduced to around 300 employees, and the future of the plant seemed grim. Due to a combination of wage freezes and staff layoffs, the remaining workforce went on strike in January 1993, eventually leading to a lockout and then the closure of the factory. This documentary, directed by Andy Twaddle, follows the developments of the strike – considered to be the last large British industrial dispute of the post-War period – as they unfolded in the early nineties. The event was heavily covered by the media at the time, and involved significant anger due to loss of livelihood and the major impact on the Dundee economy. The introduction of strikebreakers protected by police, violence on the picket line, and growing national support for striking employees, all helped to highlight just how important the factory was to the city – and how heightened emotions were at the time, given the number of jobs that were at stake.

The industrial action has since been the subject of a major exhibition at the University of Dundee, and a stage drama, *On the Line* (1996). Having garnered national attention at the time, the Timex strike became a powerful metaphor for the de-industrialisation of Scotland at the end of the century, and the documentary explains why this social event continues to evoke strong feelings even in the present day.

THE NEW SPIRIT OF WHISKY

YEAR: 2024
DIRECTOR: Michael Hilger
PRODUCTION COMPANY: NeoPOL Film

Whisky is one of Scotland's best-known exports, and the 'water of life' has been the focus of many documentaries and books over the years. *The New Spirit of Whisky* was a German-produced documentary film which sought to put a new spin on a well-established subject by spotlighting the efforts of six female protagonists – all of them either master blenders or distillery founders – who are helping to reconfigure attitudes towards the preparation, production, and sale of whisky across the country.

In the course of the documentary, the production team visited famous whisky distilleries all over Scotland, including the Nc'nean Distillery in Morvern, John Dewar & Sons in Glasgow, and the Port of Leith Distillery in Edinburgh. However, of most interest to this book was their journey to the acclaimed Arbikie Highland Estate Distillery in Montrose, Angus. This independent, family-owned distillery is considered one of the world's most sustainable, and is owned by the Stirling family – traditionally farmers since the 17th century, but who made the move into whisky after the Stirlings relocated to Lunan Bay in the 1920s. Situated in beautiful rural surroundings, the Arbikie Distillery today offers a wealth of consumer opportunities for visitors including guided whisky tours, tasting sessions, a rye experience, and even an annual whisky festival.

While in years gone by women were traditionally responsible for whisky distilling while running a family farm, this fact is often neglected, and *The New Spirit of Whisky* aims to correct misconceptions by exploring how various different female entrepreneurs have embarked upon their own business journeys to produce whisky of their own. Addressing issues such as climate change and economic challenges, they have each forged their own path to commercial success. The documentary considers the many stages that are involved in producing whisky – harvesting grain, fermentation, blending, and more – to investigate how modern distilleries balance traditional customs with technological innovation in order to promote Scotland's national drink both at home and abroad.

THE HAIRY BIKERS' BEST OF BRITISH

YEAR: 2011
DIRECTOR: Graham Dixon
PRODUCTION COMPANY: British Broadcasting Corporation

Comprised of chefs Si King and the late Dave Myers, the Hairy Bikers were (as their name suggested) both larger-than-life motorbike fanatics with a flair for cookery and good food. Between 2004 and Myers' death in 2024, the pair hosted over thirty TV series over numerous different networks, and authored a number of best-selling cookbooks. Known for their friendliness, witty banter, and approachability both on and off-screen, they were favourite fixtures on television and became celebrities in their own right.

The Hairy Bikers' Best of British was a kind of spiritual sequel to their earlier series *The Hairy Bikers' Food Tour of Britain* (2009), and was broadcast in November and December 2011 (later being re-edited into longer episodes for repeats in early 2012). The ethos of the series was for the Bikers to travel the length and breadth of the British Isles, celebrating UK food and recipes while also emphasising the importance of local produce. Naturally, given Dundee's fame as a culinary hotspot with many original dishes to its name, the city seemed like a natural destination for the pair.

The Hairy Bikers visited Dundee in episode 7 of the series, where they were to bake a Dundee Cake while on their travels. The city's famous, almond-covered traditional fruitcake, Dundee Cake has become a national favourite with a fascinating historical heritage, and the Bikers expended every effort to create the tastiest recipe possible – including customary ingredients including glace cherries and sultanas. Broadcast on the 22nd of November 2011, the episode was filmed in one of the city's most prominent and best-loved locations – the McManus Art Gallery and Museum, situated right at the heart of Dundee. This Gothic Revival building, designed by George Gilbert Scott, was opened as the Albert Institute in 1867, and was renamed in honour of Dundee's Lord Provost Maurice McManus in 2010 after a period of refurbishment. Beloved by generations of Dundonians, and by visitors far and wide, the McManus was the perfect venue for the Hairy Bikers to bake one of the city's most instantly-recognisable sweet treats, and – so affable were the eponymous presenters – the staff still speak fondly of their visit to this day.

CHILDREN OF THE CITY

YEAR: 1944
DIRECTOR: Budge Cooper
PRODUCTION COMPANY: The Scottish Office/The Ministry of Information

Children of the City is one of the most iconic documentary films about Dundee ever to be committed to celluloid. While it also featured scenes in Aberdeen and Glasgow, it is for its Dundee sequences that it has become most immediately recognised. Filmed and released during wartime, this fictionalised documentary was directed by famed film-maker Budge Cooper, and centred on the difficult topic of juvenile delinquency in Scotland at the time. The subject would have been newsworthy for contemporary viewers, given concerns that wartime conditions, evacuation, and absence of fathers due to military mobilisation were all factors that were exacerbating crime amongst minors.

The action follows a trio of young boys who are caught red-handed by Dundee police constables (played by actual policemen from the area) when they attempt to break into a pawnbroker's shop in Hilltown. The film then follows each of the boys as they are tried in a youth court, outlining the ways in which the then-new children's panels helped to establish the context around the trio's criminal actions, and explaining how attendance at approved schools might provide an effective way of correcting their future behaviour. Far from being downbeat, the entire tone of the half-hour film is actually quite optimistic, arguing that refinements in the education system, increased employment, improvements in available health services, and access to leisure-time activities could all play a part in reducing youth crime.

Today, *Children of the City* is a valuable reminder of the way in which poverty and wartime challenges affected so many youths in the 1940s. Subtitled 'a study of child delinquency in Scotland,' it was produced with an international audience in mind, and featured photography by the acclaimed Wolfgang Suschitzky, whose World War II work has since become legendary. One of his shots from the film's opening sequences is now held by the Scottish National Galleries. The film contains a strong note of social responsibility – most especially during wartime – as it stresses the need for communities to look out for each other. As an interesting aside, the mother of Dundonian boxer Dick McTaggart appears in a cameo as the parent of a child visiting a Child Guidance Clinic.

THE ROAD AND THE MILES

YEAR: 1992
DIRECTOR: Stuart Robertson
PRODUCTION COMPANY: Harrow School of Art and Technology

Productions don't always have to be epic in scope in order to pack a punch. *The Road and the Miles* (named for the traditional Scottish folk ballad, *The Road and the Miles to Dundee*, first published in 1908) featured performances by only three actors, and had a short running time. Yet it is in its evocation of time and place, as well as its raw depiction of interaction between strangers, that its action ultimately becomes most memorable.

The plot concerns George (Mark Allan, also known professionally as Mark Gilvary), who has recently returned to Dundee after a number of years working in London. His return proves to be bittersweet, however, as once back home he realises that most of his friends in the city have moved on with their lives (either literally or metaphorically), leaving him feeling isolated and adrift. Now somewhat listless, he finds himself mired in an unexpected — and increasingly surreal – love triangle with Rob (Duncan Law) and a beautiful stranger (Zita Tulyahikayo). But what exactly does the future hold for George – and has his homecoming really been all that he had hoped for?

With sequences filmed both in London and Dundee, *The Road and the Miles* makes the most of its shoestring budget to set up a genuinely intriguing premise – one which plays out in surprising and unexpected ways. Like the song from which the drama takes its name, there is a sense of fleeting acquaintance and febrile experience. While the lyrics describe a man meeting and offering to accompany a woman who seeks to get to Dundee – and becoming attracted to her, even though he realises they will almost certainly never meet again – so too the film depicts complex dynamics between acquaintances which underscore the intricacy and unpredictability of human relationships.

It can be sometimes be challenging for a short film to build suspense effectively, and yet *The Road and the Miles* has a tendency to juxtapose the recognisable and the unfamiliar to discomfiting effect. It may not be a box-office blockbuster, but in terms of urban mystery it is never less than thought-provoking.

BOB SERVANT, INDEPENDENT

YEAR: 2013-14
DIRECTORS: Annie Griffin and Simon Hynd
PRODUCTION COMPANY: British Broadcasting Corporation

Bob Servant has become one of Scotland's best-known comedy characters of recent years, due in no small part to the talents of international acting talent Brian Cox – among Dundee's favourite sons. The Bob Servant story began with a series of novels by author, screenwriter, and journalist Neil Forsyth, and led to a radio adaptation in 2012 (*The Bob Servant Emails*) which would feature many of the stars of the TV series. Sure enough, the character was soon brought to life on the small screen, with filming taking place on *Bob Servant, Independent* throughout 2012 in locations around Glasgow and Dundee.

The storyline follows an unexpected by-election in the inimitable Dundee suburb of Broughty Ferry, when the sitting MP is shockingly decapitated in a car accident. To the surprise of many in the town, Bob Servant (Brian Cox) – a local fast-food salesman renowned for his cheeseburger vans – decides to throw his hat into the ring as an independent candidate for parliament. Not least flabbergasted is his unconventional assistant, Frank (Jonathan Watson), who suddenly finds himself thrust into the role of campaign manager. Servant faces an uphill struggle against a highly polished political opponent, Nick Edwards (Rufus Jones), and his lifelong nemesis Hendo (Alex Norton).

The series made great use of the beautiful surroundings of Broughty Ferry, and its comedic content was hugely enhanced by the involvement of some remarkable Scottish actors in supporting roles, including Derek Riddell, Shirley Henderson, Greg McHugh, and Sanjeev Kohli. The show was a success with many critics, and went straight to a network broadcast – being first transmitted on BBC4 before being repeated on BBC2 Scotland. *Bob Servant, Independent* was nominated for a Scottish BAFTA Award and a Royal Television Society Comedy Award, and was renewed for a second series (this time entitled simply *Bob Servant*) which was broadcast in 2014. The continuation followed Bob and Frank through the post-election aftermath in Broughty Ferry, and included some romantic entanglements for both characters. It proved successful with audiences and critics alike, and won the Royal Television Society Scotland Comedy Award.

STONE OF DESTINY

YEAR: 2008
DIRECTOR: Charles Martin Smith
PRODUCTION COMPANY: Infinity Films Entertainment/The Mob Film Company

The tale of Scotland's ancient royal coronation stone, the Stone of Scone – captured by England's King Edward I in 1296 before being stolen back in 1950, following a heist that captivated the nation – is a story that has often stimulated the imagination of audiences. American writer-director Charles Martin Smith decided to retell this famous story for the big screen in 2008, drawing on considerable acting talent to bring the daring raid to life and using many of the original real-life locations involved in the Stone's liberation.

Stone of Destiny centres on the efforts of Scottish Covenant Association member Ian Hamilton (Charlie Cox) to achieve home rule, only to find both parliament and the general public to be largely apathetic to his cause. Undeterred, he and his friend Bill Craig (Billy Boyd) hatch a plan in 1950 to steal the Stone of Destiny from its current location at Westminster Abbey. They painstakingly plan the heist, but Craig takes cold feet and withdraws. Hamilton is later introduced, through prominent devolution campaigner John MacCormick (Robert Carlyle), to activists Kay Matheson (Kate Mara) and Gavin Vernon (Stephen McCole). Together with driver Alan Stuart (Ciaron Kelly), they choose Christmas Eve to break into Westminster Abbey – using the distraction of the festivities to cover their tracks – but face many struggles before they are finally in a position to retrieve the stone. After many diversions and evasions, the students eventually return the stone to Scotland, but realise that it may become damaged if left to the elements. To ensure its survival, they take it to Arbroath Abbey – a location significant to Scotland's self-determination as a nation – and surrender it to the authorities. While the conspirators are arrested, they are ultimately never prosecuted, and the stone is returned to London.

Smith's feature made excellent use of Scottish location filming, including at the University of Glasgow, Paisley Abbey, and the Glenfinnan Viaduct. However, it is for its atmospheric evocation of Arbroath Abbey in the climactic scenes that it has arguably become best remembered. The expansive supporting cast included actors Juliet Cadzow, Peter Mullan, and Brenda Fricker.

GO DOWN SWINGING

YEAR: 2018
DIRECTOR: Various Directors
PRODUCTION COMPANY: Golf Films

Carnoustie is renowned not only for being the home of golf in Angus – its amazing reputation extends right across Scotland, and to the wider world beyond. *Go Down Swinging* is a sporting documentary which recounts the nail-bitingly sudden shift in fortune at the 128th Open Championship in 1999 when golfer Jean van de Velde – seemingly destined to win the title – used up a three-shot lead on the 18th hole, and then eventually lost the tournament in a play-off. The event is now considered one of the most memorable collapses in any modern golf major.

Premiering on 9th July 2018 on the Golf Channel, *Go Down Swinging* brought to life this suspenseful turn of events, with participation from sporting figures such as Paul Lawrie (the eventual winner of the tournament), Mike Tirico, Peter Alliss, and Justin Leonard, as well as van de Velde himself. Filmed on location at the immaculately-maintained Carnoustie Golf Links, the documentary draws on a variety of interviews to pinpoint exactly what happened at that fateful Open Championship, asking how van de Velde eventually – and quite literally – snatched defeat from the jaws of victory.

With a wide range of detailed and candid interviews, *Go Down Swinging* is a must-see for any golfing connoisseur, featuring original broadcast footage alongside first-person accounts of the remarkable twist in fate that occurred. (Even van de Velde's caddy, Christophe Angiolini, is interviewed as a witness to events.) Comedian Lenny Clarke adds some much-needed light relief to proceedings by portraying a fictional bartender who narrates the action to the audience as it unfolds and explains just how remarkable this sporting moment really was.

Carnoustie Championship Course is well-regarded the world over as one of the most challenging golf courses, and during the 1999 Open the conditions of play were regarded as especially brutal. This documentary pinpoints exactly what happened on that fateful day of the final, and explores the full spectrum of emotions that were involved.

THE OPEN ROAD TRIP

YEAR: 2022
DIRECTOR: Jamie Weir
PRODUCTION COMPANY: Sky Studios

Always in demand both as a sporting destination and a beloved tourist location, Carnoustie also featured in Sky Sports' documentary mini-series *The Open Road Trip*, which was broadcast in five parts starting on 4th July 2022. Presented by Sky Sports News reporter and golf correspondent Jamie Weir, the series ambitiously set out to explore every Championship venue to have ever hosted The Open (past and present), in advance of that year's 150th Open which took place at St Andrews Old Course.

Joining the indefatigable Weir on his journey was his friend and cameraman Chris Johnson. The pair travelled to fourteen Championship courses in all, including Royal Portush, Royal St George's, Royal Birkdale, Royal Troon, and – of course – Carnoustie. Not only did he go in search of the best stories surrounding the Open in each venue, but – being an avid golfing enthusiast himself – he played a hole on every course he visited against someone who had a particular connection to either the location or the Championship.

Alongside archive coverage and brand new footage of these iconic courses, Weir found himself joined by fellow admirers of the Claret Jug such as acclaimed actor James Nesbitt and numerous sporting figures including Gary Player, Paul Lawrie, Mairi Pollock, Ken Goodwin, Andrew Coltart, and many others. At each location, he discusses not just the link between the course and the Open Championship, but many other tales of interest surrounding every one of these significant locations.

While featuring fourteen of the most famous golf courses on the planet over just five episodes of TV may seem like an impossibly bold aim, Weir is a likeable host, and – together with his guests – he manages to cover an impressive amount of ground (both geographically and in terms of subject matter). Fans of Carnoustie will not be disappointed by his enthusiastic exploration of the Golf Links; given that 'Golf's Greatest Test' has hosted The Open on eight occasions to date (between 1931 and 2018), it more than earns its place in this wide-ranging documentary.

CHRISTABEL

YEAR: 1988
DIRECTOR: Adrian Shergold
PRODUCTION COMPANY: British Broadcasting Corporation

Dennis Potter was one of the great British post-war TV dramatists, and he was at the height of his powers when he adapted Christabel Bielenberg's autobiographical book *The Past is Myself* (1968) for BBC TV. Broadcast between 16th November and 7th December 1988, *Christabel* follows the life of the aforementioned British writer over the years 1932–45 when she was living in Nazi Germany in the approach to, and throughout, the Second World War. Today, the series is particularly well remembered as being an early starring role for Elizabeth Hurley, who would go on to international fame in films such as *Austin Powers: International Man of Mystery* (1997) and *Bedazzled* (2000).

The miniseries explored the human side of the horrors of war by following young English writer Christabel Burton (Hurley) as she marries lawyer Peter Bielenberg (Stephen Dillane) and moves with him to Germany to make their home together. Her father (Geoffrey Palmer) has grave misgivings about their relocation to the continent from the start, and he is soon proven right when the Nazis come to power and the young couple discover the authoritarian terror and callous disregard for human life that is to come. As the march to war begins, the Bielenbergs become increasingly desperate to cling on to basic human dignity as the true terror of the Nazis' barbaric political intentions become clear. Ultimately, what began as a dawning realisation of widespread danger soon becomes a full-blown battle just to survive.

While *Christabel* was filmed across a range of destinations throughout Budapest in Hungary and Villach in Austria, as well as Dorset in England, it also made extensive use of Dundee as a filming location. Of particular note was the employment of the grand exterior of Dundee High School, designed by architect George Angus and built in 1824. Meanwhile, 1940s inner-city Berlin was recreated at the Camperdown Works in Lochee, once the world's largest jute mill complex, which was closed in 1981 but used to great effect in the filming of *Christabel* prior to its eventual demolition and redevelopment a few years later.

SILENT WITNESS: IN A LONELY PLACE

YEAR: 2014
DIRECTOR: Craig Viveiros
PRODUCTION COMPANY: BBC Studios Drama Productions

The long-running BBC crime drama *Silent Witness* has been entertaining audiences since 1996 and – at time of writing – has spanned a remarkable 28 series and 248 episodes. Created by Nigel McCrery and initially starring Amanda Burton, *Silent Witness* has been headlined by Emilia Fox since 2004. Featuring the investigations of a police forensic pathology unit, the series has never flinched from graphic depictions of grisly crime, often including extreme violence and murder.

Broadcast in two parts, on the 16th and 17th January 2014 respectively, *Silent Witness: In a Lonely Place* saw the show's stars – forensic pathologist Dr Nikki Alexander (Emilia Fox) and scientist Jack Hodgson (David Caves) – travel to Scotland to assist police enquiries following the discovery of a young woman's body in a secluded rural area. Working with the local police, the pathologists soon uncover the work of a serial killer, and the investigations soon converge on a mysterious private club where nothing is quite as it seems. Eventually, unexpected connections begin to emerge which implicate the least expected of figures, and Alexander and Hodgson must push their investigative skills to the limit in order to eventually unmask the murderer.

An atmospheric tale which shines an uncomfortable light on obsession and violence, *In a Lonely Place* made highly effective use of its location filming, with scenes set around the Tay Road Bridge (which, at 2,250 metres long, is one of the longest road bridges in Europe), venues throughout the city of Dundee, and the Angus Glens. The rural settings provided the remote backdrop for the hidden location of the murderer's blood-soaked attempts to obfuscate their brutal killings, while the famous Taxi Club in Stirling Street was used to create a moody exterior. Even more striking were panoramic views of Dundee taken from Law Hill, where wide landscape shots gave a sense of scale to proceedings and emphasised the fact that the characters were far removed from their usual London stomping ground – and were facing a different set of challenges.

TRACES

YEAR: 2019-22
DIRECTORS: Mary Nighy, Chris Foggin and Claire Winyard
PRODUCTION COMPANY: Red Production Company (a StudioCanal Company)

Tartan Noir crime stories have long been one of Scotland's most greatly prized creative exports, and *Traces* was a suspenseful addition to the genre. Co-created and co-written by Amelia Bullmore and Scottish crime writing legend Val McDermid, and based on an original premise by McDermid, *Traces* was a fascinatingly multi-layered exploration of forensic pathology in relation to an increasingly complex murder case.

Set in Dundee, though largely filmed in Bolton and Manchester, the action of *Traces* mainly took place in the fictitious Scottish Institute of Forensic Science and Anatomy, based at the (equally fictional) University of Tayside. Heading the cast of characters were chemist Professor Sarah Gordon (Laura Fraser), forensic anthropologist Professor Kathy Torrence (Jennifer Spence), and laboratory technician Emma Hedges (Molly Windsor), who has recently relocated back to Dundee in search of answers relating to the long-ago murder of her mother on the Law Hill. The supporting cast also included a wide range of Scottish acting talent, including Martin Compston, John Gordon Sinclair, Neve McIntosh, Michael Nardone, and the late comedian Janey Godley as criminal defence lawyer Clare Tindall.

Traces followed the central cast of highly-trained professionals as they used their extensive scientific skills to identify and track down murderers. While the first series closely followed Emma's harrowing personal and professional journey as she attempts to track down her late mother's killer, the second series chronicled an equally nail-biting investigation as the team races to track down the perpetrator of a series of deadly bombings – brought about using deviously-improvised explosive devices – in locations across Dundee before the culprit can strike again. Both series of the drama were broadcast on the Alibi channel – the first between the 9th and 24th December 2019, and the second between the 15th February and 22nd March 2022 – and both were later repeated on BBC TV.

While the series was set in and around Dundee, actual location filming there turned out to be brief, with numerous members of the cast remarking in interviews that they were surprised (and often disappointed) that they hadn't been required to spend time in the the city itself during the production. The centrally-located cities of Manchester and Bolton were instead chosen to provide a wide range of urban, suburban, and rural scenes as required by the narrative. These included everything from city centre commercial locations to parks, residential venues, and many other inner-city properties.

Among the Dundee locations and landmarks visible throughout the series were the Tay Road Bridge, the famous Desperate Dan statue in the High Street (the larger-than-life character being a legendary figure from D.C. Thomson's long-running *The Dandy* comic), Caird Hall and the City Square, Reform Street, Chandlers Lane, Wellington Street, and Dundee Law – once more being used for its commanding views of the surrounding area. The scientific department which is the focus of the series, the Scottish Institute of Forensic Science and Anatomy, is widely thought to have been inspired by the world-renowned, real-life Leverhulme Research Centre for Forensic Science located at the University of Dundee. The director of the Leverhulme Research Centre, Professor Niamh Nic Daeid, was an advisor on *Traces* and helped to ensure the accuracy of the characters' investigative methods as well as the technical content of their dialogue.

While filming in Dundee was brief, the city still took *Traces* to its heart, and the series has become one of the more famous evocations of the city to appear in a TV production in recent years. Photos of the series' stars during filming were featured in the local press, and it quickly developed a following with the public. The series was praised for its fidelity to real forensic procedures and its charting of protagonist Emma Hedges' progression from trainee lab technician to an apprentice forensic chemist, demonstrating the character's skill and tenacity in developing her career in spite of the many traumatic events (and surprising plot twists) that she encounters along the way.

Traces may not be among the most famous work of the creatively productive Val McDermid, but it certainly made a positive impact on account of its strong performances (especially from lead actor Molly Windsor), compelling storylines, and detailed portrayal of the science behind forensic pathology.

SPOOKED: SCOTLAND

YEAR: 2022
DIRECTORS: Daniel Edwards, Chris McMillan and Benjie Bateman
PRODUCTION COMPANY: Tern TV/Discovery+

Paranormal investigation documentary *Spooked: Scotland* covered numerous different destinations around the country, using a variety of detection techniques to determine whether supernatural activity was taking place in or around particular venues. Fronted by model and TV presenter Gail Porter, the series purported to focus on the most reportedly haunted locations in Scotland, and was streamed on HBO Max. Porter was joined on her travels by American psychic medium Chris Fleming, who attempted to make contact with supernatural entities as part of the investigations in each place they encountered.

Among the Scottish destinations the series would focus on were the Tron Theatre in Glasgow, Culross Palace in Fife, the Vaults of Edinburgh Old Town, Castle Menzies in Perthshire, and numerous others. One prominent Dundonian site visited by the series was the famous Verdant Works Museum, a painstakingly-restored mill on West Henderson's Wynd housing acclaimed historical displays which recount the story of jute production throughout the 19th and 20th centuries, which has won its custodians, Dundee Heritage Trust, universal praise amongst cultural commentators and the public alike.

Spooked: Scotland brought an aspect of reality TV immediacy to paranormal science, a subject which is often controversial and perennially debated. The team investigated different areas of the Verdant Works site, where hazardous working conditions in the Victorian era had led to frequent employee casualties – leading to later reports of spectral children (who had fallen victim to industrial deaths) still frequenting the premises. As their research unfolds, viewers discover that while jute manufacturing could be a lucrative business, it was not without risk for the workforce involved in its production.

The documentary series was followed a year later by the similarly-themed *Spooked: Ireland*, with Porter being succeeded by Vogue Williams as presenter. The sequel series investigated many historic Irish destinations such as Ardgillan Castle, Wicklow Jail, and Blackwater Castle, looking into supernatural disturbances at each venue.

DON'T LET THE DEVIL TAKE ANOTHER DAY

YEAR: 2020
DIRECTOR: Ben Lowe
PRODUCTION COMPANY: Peachalabama Ltd.

Don't Let the Devil Take Another Day was a live album by Kelly Jones, frontman of Welsh rock band Stereophonics, and featured 21 tracks which were recorded in a wide range of different locations during his solo tour in 2019. A documentary of the same name, which followed Jones throughout the production of the album, was recorded simultaneously and released in 2020. The film followed performances by Jones in famed venues all around the world, from London to San Francisco via Blackpool and Llandudno. Scottish destinations he visited included the Glasgow Royal Concert Hall in Sauchiehall Street, and – of course – the irreplaceable Caird Hall in Dundee.

While, on the face of it, the documentary sought to present Jones' performances from the album by using footage from the plethora of different destinations he had visited on his tour, the scope of the narrative was broadened significantly when doctors diagnosed a vocal polyp which had to be surgically removed from Jones' throat, emphasising the degree of uncertainty this created due to the very real possibility that it would subsequently impact on his ability for musical performance. With frank honesty, his sense of vulnerability as an artist is explored in detail, closely following his trepidation about returning to performing live after the procedure had taken place, and culminating in the triumph of overcoming this setback to complete the tour.

As mentioned, the Caird Hall is just one of the locations in which Jones would perform, and the charged atmosphere is palpable. The documentary recounts a rarefied moment in music performance, due to its production directly proceeding the coronavirus pandemic lockdowns of 2020 and 2021, forcing many in the industry to consider the economic and artistic impact that came from being unable to host public gigs during this period. The film was praised for its sincerity, with Jones's self-produced video diaries supplementing the action and providing a unique view into the creative process from a truly distinctive recording artist.

AS YOU LIKE IT

YEAR: 1978
DIRECTOR: Basil Coleman
PRODUCTION COMPANY: British Broadcasting Corporation

The BBC Television Shakespeare was an ambitious series of television adaptations of all 37 of William Shakespeare's plays, produced between 1978 and 1985, which featured performances by some of British acting's big hitters of the time. This included Derek Jacobi as Hamlet, Charles Gray as Julius Caesar, and Nicol Williamson as Macbeth. The series has been widely repeated and released on home entertainment formats in the years since its broadcast, not least as an educational aid, and helped to make The Bard's material significantly more accessible for modern audiences of the time.

Airing on 17th December 1978, *As You Like It* was filmed on the expansive grounds of Glamis Castle in Angus, and proved to be one of only two of the *BBC Television Shakespeare* plays to be shot on location (the other being *Henry VIII* the following year). This led to criticism that it deviated from the productions of Shakespeare's time, where the action would have played out in a much more theatrical setting – an atmosphere which was challenged by the presence of the natural world in the final broadcast product.

While director Basil Coleman had initially anticipated filming the production alongside the changing of the seasons, scheduling constraints meant that he instead had to shoot the production entirely within the month of May, which presented further challenges when it came to depicting the gradual changing of the environment. The action faithfully follows Shakespeare's original play, with the Forest of Arden's inhabitants including the deposed Duke Senior (Tony Church); his estranged daughter Rosalind (Helen Mirren); and her inept suitor, Orlando (Brian Stirner). As always, there are misunderstandings, love poetry, and even the unexpected presence of a lion, before true love can prevail.

The series was the brainchild of producer Cedric Messina, who had been so inspired by the grandeur of Glamis Castle when filming *The Little Minister* in 1975 that he resolved to return for this retelling of the famous Shakespearean comedy. It also marked the triumphant return of Helen Mirren to the Castle after her earlier role in the aforementioned drama.

LENNY GOES TO TOWN

YEAR: 1998
DIRECTOR: John L. Spencer
PRODUCTION COMPANY: Crucial Films/British Broadcasting Corporation

Actor and stand-up comedian Lenny Henry took to the road for this unconventional six-part travelogue, where he visited towns and cities across the UK to perform a comedy show in each location. These included venues in Stoke on Trent, Port Talbot, Cambridge, Brighton, and Northampton. However, his show was not to be entirely devoid of Scottish destinations, as the final episode saw him treading the boards in Dundee.

Airing on the 10th of October 1998, the sixth episode of *Lenny Goes to Town* saw the ebullient Henry – with his trademark lightning-fast wit – taking to the stage while also being involved in a variety of cutaway visits to destinations around Tayside. The show additionally allowed him to appear in the guise of some of his comedy characters, usually with uproarious results. There was also a parodic quiz show element, offering an unsuspecting member of the public a prize if they were brave enough to try their luck at winning it.

Lenny Henry's usual mix of sharp intellect and zany humour made for a trip to Dundee that was never less than entertaining, and he investigates the city's growing reputation for computer game design (being the home of games as varied as *Lemmings* and *Grand Theft Auto*). He also discovers what makes the city such a distinctive place by immersing himself in the local culture, approving of its unique venues and outgoing people.

Lenny Goes to Town was a series packed full of celebrity appearances, often in deeply unexpected roles, including *The League of Gentlemen*'s Mark Gatiss, Steve Pemberton, and Reece Shearsmith; Jerry Hall; Robbie Williams; Mick Hucknall; Gary Lineker; and *Red Dwarf*'s Hattie Hayridge, amongst many others. While the programme is rarely remembered these days (largely on account of its brief run), it offered an excellent showcase for Henry's diverse performance talents, and also presents a distinctive glimpse of Dundee at a time of great transition in the late 1990s.

THE PARTY

YEAR: 2002
DIRECTOR: Mikail Chowdhury
PRODUCTION COMPANY: Spontinuity Productions

A comic drama with the idiosyncrasies of undergraduate life well and truly in its sights, *The Party* was the brainchild of Mikail Chowdhury – an early work which would foreshadow his later, Emmy-nominated career as a producer, and also as a versatile screenwriter, playwright, and director (for which he has also won awards).

Centring on scenes at the University of Dundee and the wider city, the film follows a group of friends nearing the end of student life. In the approach to graduation, student Paul (Chris Bettiss) decides on impulse that he will hold one final party before all of his friends go on their separate ways. Rather than being simply an altruistic gesture, his efforts have an alternative motive: to spark a romance with the beautiful Susan (Kate Ackroyd) before the opportunity passes them by. But the path of true love never did run smooth, and his university pals – sometimes well-meaning, sometimes erratic, and sometimes outright interfering – seem more intent on thwarting his plans than aiding them.

With a supporting cast headlined by actors including Daniel Conroy and Sarah Natali, *The Party* lives up to its stated intention of exploring the matters that are really at the forefront of the minds of young adults who – their higher education studies now completed – are facing the prospect of a life of work and responsibility following their comparatively carefree time as undergraduates. The film was certainly a showcase for the work of the creatively resourceful Chowdhury, who – in addition to being its director and writer – was responsible for its editing, cinematography, and sound. (He even appears in the brief role of Simon.) The original score was composed by Stuart Cattanach.

The Party premiered at the New York International Film and Video Festival, and screened in cities as varied as Los Angeles and Las Vegas. The film was shot entirely on location in Dundee, using equipment from the Dundee Digital Resource, and was later screened at the Dundee Contemporary Arts Centre.

MARTIN COMPSTON'S SCOTTISH FLING

YEAR: 2022
DIRECTOR: Rod Tamime
PRODUCTION COMPANY: Tern TV/BBC Scotland

Scottish actor Martin Compston, well-known to audiences for his roles in dramas such as *Line of Duty* and *Mary, Queen of Scots*, got the chance to reveal his lighter side in this travel miniseries. *Martin Compston's Scottish Fling* saw the intense performer become a genial presenter as he and his friend Phil MacHugh visited locations all across Scotland to see what is most remarkable about the country in the modern age, as well as checking out as many outdoor activities as possible along the way.

In the third episode of the series, broadcast on 22nd September 2022, Compston and MacHugh visit Abertay University to discover how Dundee has become a world-leading centre for videogame development. With its pioneering role in the subject, strong industry connections, and its specialised curriculum, Abertay University was the first university in the world to offer a dedicated degree in computer game design back in 1997. With Dundee having been an acknowledged industry hotspot for videogames in the 1990s and 2000s thanks to companies such as DMA Design/Rockstar North and Realtime Worlds, it seemed like the ideal location for Abertay's global success in providing higher education on the subject, and it has since cemented its reputation as a global leader in the field.

Later in the episode, the presenters visit Arbroath to sample the legendary smokies – a wood-smoked haddock delicacy – and discover how they are prepared and sold to thousands of visitors to the area every year. The fish are prepared using a time-honoured, traditional method which has remained unchanged for centuries, and are prized for their distinctive taste and aroma. Arbroath Smokies have been awarded Protected Geographical Indication status under European Law, meaning that they can only use that particular name if they are produced within a five-mile radius of the town of Arbroath.

Compston and MacHugh visited many different parts of Scotland on their travels – from the Western Isles to Aberdeen – and present a very upbeat and contemporary take on the nation's traditions and innovations which is refreshingly buoyant.

JUTE CITY

YEAR: 1991
DIRECTOR: Stuart Orme
PRODUCTION COMPANY: British Broadcasting Corporation

Jute City was an intricate three-part thriller broadcast on the BBC between 27th October and 10th November 1991, filmed primarily in Dundee and Ullapool in the Highlands. Centring around murky underworld dealings, the series featured an array of top acting talent including Joanna Roth, Clive Russell, John Sessions, Phyllis Calvert, and Peter Mullan, and made the most of its shadowy urban Tayside setting.

The story involved a successful economist named Duncan Kerr (David O'Hara), who had briefly returned to his home city of Dundee to celebrate the wedding of his brother, Sammy (Douglas Henshall). All does not go well at the stag night, however, with various disagreeable characters crossing Duncan's path, and in a shocking twist Sammy's corpse is later discovered. As events unfold, it becomes clear that the murdered Sammy had been responsible for hoarding and laundering illicit funds – but for whom? Duncan soon discovers that he must stay at least three steps ahead of everyone else if he is to survive his off-the-books investigations as the body count begins to pile up, a conspiracy involving toxic waste begins to emerge, and some deadly figures become implicated in the intrigue.

Jute City skilfully – and at times mercilessly – ratcheted up the suspense over the course of its run, thanks in no small part to David Kane's tightly-written screenplays and some stellar performances. The miniseries drew in everything from fictional corruption to environmental issues as part of its central mystery, and generally performed well with the critics of the time. With a dark but genuinely unexpected *denouement*, and some excellent filming in and around Dundee, *Jute City* skilfully took its place alongside other grittily uncompromising Tartan Noir mysteries of the time.

In a further, interesting Scottish connection, Dave Stewart of the Eurythmics composed the original score for the miniseries, and that same year would release an album of the soundtrack under the name David A. Stewart.

BRIAN COX'S JUTE JOURNEY

YEAR: 2009
DIRECTOR: Brian Ross
PRODUCTION COMPANY: Hopscotch Films/British Broadcasting Corporation

Dundee-born actor Brian Cox has become a beloved figure in his home city, and in this documentary he took a personal look at the impact of the jute trade on its history. Cox's parents began their working lives in the jute industry, making him an ideal figure to examine the centrality of its manufacture in the nineteenth and twentieth centuries. Jute production created a rough, shiny bast fibre – which could be spun into strong threads – from the flowering *Corchorus* plants which grow plentifully in countries such as Bangladesh and India. This traditionally linked Dundee with the Indian city of Kolkata in particular, where jute was called 'the golden fibre' and had been hand-crafted there for centuries.

Broadcast on the 5th of October 2009, this one hour feature saw Cox following the stories of past Dundonians who had relocated to Kolkata to work in the Indian jute industry, and considered the vast impact of the material on Dundee – and the world – during the heyday of its manufacture. Far from idealising the past, however, he also explores the industrial risk to jute workers over the years, and discusses how its production advanced from a hand-made technique through to a machine-workable process (initially with the application of whale oil). Additionally, he reveals the way in which Dundee's manufacturing industry was transformed overnight by this versatile material, which was responsible for everything from weaving Hessian sacks to tarpaulin and rope.

The population of Dundee quadrupled as a result of the booming jute market, drawing in workers from far and wide, and – along with jam and journalism – it remains one of the most instantly recognisable aspects for which the city was historically best-known. Cox considers not just the transformation brought about in the city, but also the lasting legacy that the jute trade has left on its cultural heritage. He draws upon his own experiences to add an individual perspective to the documentary, showing audiences not just the distinguished, world-famous actor that the public knows but also – by reflecting on his past involvement with the city – a more introspective and contemplative side.

SUCCESSION

YEAR: 2019
DIRECTOR: Kevin Bray
PRODUCTION COMPANY: HBO Entertainment/Gary Sanchez Productions/ Hyperobject Industries/Hot Seat Productions/Project Zeus

A wildly successful satirical comedy-drama TV series which ran between June 2018 and May 2023, *Succession* was broadcast on HBO and soon earned international acclaim. Headlined by Brian Cox as media mogul patriarch Logan Roy, the series centred around the internecine manoeuvring of Roy's four children – Connor (Alan Ruck), Kendall (Jeremy Strong), Roman (Kieran Culkin), and Shiv (Sarah Snook) – as they prepared to take on the mantle of the family's company, entertainment multinational Waystar RoyCo, in the event of their father's eventual demise. A winner of numerous industry awards including Golden Globes, Primetime Emmys, and BAFTAs, the series won much praise for its dark humour, elaborate plots, and astute dialogue.

Of most interest to this book from the series' 39 episodes was 'Dundee,' which aired on the 29th of September 2019. Written by Mary Laws and directed by Kevin Bray, the story revolved around Logan – a self-made man who grew up in poverty in Dundee – overseeing the celebrations for the 50th anniversary of Waystar RoyCo which are set to take place in the city. As the action of *Succession* was largely set in and around New York, the sudden shift to Tayside was visually striking, and location filming took place near the RRS *Discovery* and the then-newly-opened V&A Dundee Museum. The well-to-do family are also seen staying at the globally-renowned Gleneagles Hotel near Auchterarder in Perthshire.

This episode was praised amongst fans of the show for the way in which it broadened and deepened understanding of Logan Roy's character – as always, perfectly articulated by Dundee's own Brian Cox – and it also featured the establishment of the fictional Logan Roy School of Journalism. It is, arguably, best remembered amongst Scots for the scenes filmed in and around the eye-catching V&A Dundee building; designed by architect Kengo Kuma and opened on the 15th of September 2018 by Prince William, Duke of Cambridge and Catherine, Duchess of Cambridge, the museum has become one of the most instantly-recognisable locations in the city, and by its fifth anniversary had been visited by 1.7 million people, contributing £109 million to Dundee's economy.

BILLY MACKENZIE: THE GLAMOUR CHASE

YEAR: 2000
DIRECTOR: Andrew Miller
PRODUCTION COMPANY: Voyager Television/Scottish Television Enterprises

Co-founder and lead vocalist of pop band The Associates, Billy Mackenzie was a distinctive figure who was widely recognised for his high tenor voice and versatile songwriting talents. Born in Dundee and raised in the city's Stobswell district, he travelled widely throughout countries such as New Zealand and the United States before returning to Scotland and founding a band with guitarist Alan Rankine in 1976, initially called the Ascorbic Ones and Mental Torture before eventually settling on the name The Associates in 1979. While Rankine departed the group in 1982, Mackenzie continued to perform under The Associates name until the early nineties, when he started using his own name to release work such as his studio album *Outernational* (1992).

Commissioned by Scottish Television Enterprises and produced by Voyager Television, *Billy Mackenzie: The Glamour Chase* is a documentary directed by Andrew Miller which sought to shine a light on Mackenzie's all-too-brief career (the artist died in 1997, aged only 39) and explain his contribution to post-punk, synth-pop, and experimental pop, as well as the new wave. Though filmed on a very modest budget, the feature included interviews from numerous prominent figures in the music industry of the time, such as Marc Almond, Siouxsie Sioux, and Martin Fry. Using archive footage and the input of Mackenzie's biographer Tom Doyle, the documentary pieces together a picture of a complex but brilliant talent. As well as being filmed in the singer's native Dundee, sequences were also shot in Switzerland, Edinburgh, and London.

Two versions of *The Glamour Chase* have been released: a 23 minute cut which was broadcast on STV in June 2000, and subsequently a longer 45 minute cut (considered the definitive version) which was released online. With contributions from Mackenzie's family and members of bands such as Yello, Heaven 17, and Apollo 440, the documentary elaborates on the formative influences which helped to shape such a unique musical talent before considering his wider impact on the industry of the time, delineating a figure who was simultaneously fearlessly maverick and boundlessly creative.

CHRISTMAS IN THE SCHEMES (MUSIC VIDEO)

YEAR: 2019
DIRECTOR: Graeme Robertson
PRODUCTION COMPANY: SeaGate Studio

The Cundeez (the Dundonian vernacular term for manhole covers) are an inimitable Scottish punk rock band based in Dundee who describe their style as 'Skeem Rock' – a tip of the hat to the fact that many of their songs centre on the experience of growing up in Dundee's housing projects, otherwise known as 'the schemes.' Established in 2007, the band's members include Stevie Cundee; Trotsky Cundee; Tez 'The Cockney' Cundee; and lead vocalist/bagpiper Gary Robertson, who is also active as a poet and author. Known as 'Dundee's Street Poet,' Robertson was the first winner of the BBC reality show/contest *SAS: Are You Tough Enough?* in 2002, and has written widely on under-explored aspects of life in the city such as *Gangs of Dundee* (2008), an evaluation of city gang culture from the 1960s onwards, and *Skeem Life: Growing Up in the Seventies* (2010) which detailed the experience of adolescent life in a then-new Dundee housing scheme.

Never knowingly taking themselves too seriously, The Cundeez have achieved cult fame in Dundee and beyond, and their music video for *Christmas in the Schemes*, released in 2019, reflects on festive season celebrations of yesteryear – all taking place in an old-school Dundonian living room with an invitingly roaring fire. The result is a warm and nostalgic look back through the years, including archive footage of young Gary Robertson opening gifts with his family (including a brand new bike and board game *KerPlunk*) as well as – in the present day – receiving the very pinnacle of Dundee Christmas presents, *Oor Wullie* and *The Broons* annuals (as published every year by the city's D.C. Thomson and enjoyed by readers worldwide).

The track was written by Gary Robertson and Stevie Cundee, and was initially released on CD around 2008. However, with the growing influence of social media, the band decided years later to produce a music video for distribution over the Internet to their many fans across the globe. With its evocation of a seventies family Christmas, complete with period decorations and original visual snippets of the Whitfield multis, *Christmas in the Schemes* conjures up a unique Yuletide celebration that could only have been produced in Dundee.

MIA (MUSIC VIDEO)

YEAR: 2016
DIRECTOR: Lindsay Brown
PRODUCTION COMPANY: Stray Seal

Singer Nicola Madill has won high praise for her emotionally touching songwriting and her hauntingly atmospheric vocals, with critics enthusing about the uncompromisingly honest storytelling and rich symbolism evident in her albums *Selene* (2017) and *Absentee* (2025). She has toured widely as a live performance artist, having made appearances in venues as far-ranging as the Cavern Pub in Liverpool, the Gulbenkian Arts Centre in Canterbury, and the Globe in Cardiff.

One of Madill's most memorable music videos was the visually striking accompaniment to her song *Mia*, which was shot by director Lindsay Brown in 2016. The singer had been inspired to create a sub-aquatic feature by her experiences of looking over the water from Tayside, considering not just the River Tay but also the North Sea into which it flows, and found a natural collaborator in Fife-based film-maker Brown, who had gained experience of diving with the British Sub-Aqua Club some years earlier.

In addition to providing the artistic direction for the video, Brown was also able to supply practical advice on underwater movement to Madill as well as guiding the other actors (experienced divers from BSAC) who were participating in the feature. Filming took place at Dundee and Angus College, at a swimming pool on campus, and presented numerous technical challenges including the arrangement of effective lighting for each shot, the choreography of each moving figure, and the effectiveness of the costumes.

The production of the *Mia* music video was aided by a crowdfunding campaign, and the ambitious project involved an eight week preparation period in order for all of the arrangements for the filming to be in place prior to the actual shoot. While Madill was already an experienced swimmer prior to the production, she sought additional advice on holding her breath for prolonged periods as well as instruction on buoyancy while moving underwater. The finished product was a very impressive demonstration of what can be possible when a very clear creative vision is put into practice by an experienced production team.

OPEN CLOSE MOVIE

YEAR: 2018
DIRECTOR: Jon Gill
PRODUCTION COMPANY: Playful Communications

Open Close Movie was a tremendously aspirational project which sought to document the creation of two unique street art trails in Dundee in the period leading up to the highly-anticipated establishment of the V&A Museum on Riverside Esplanade. Filmed entirely on a mobile device by director Jon Gill, the ethos of this hour-long documentary feature seemed to be in direct creative juxtaposition to the the newsworthy events surrounding it – the V&A Dundee was a development of enormous significance for the city, both logistically and culturally, so why would this particular moment in history present a favourable opportunity to establish not one but two community-led collections of urban artwork at the grass-roots level?

Gill's decision to record the action of *Open Close Movie* on a mobile device certainly added to the feature's sense of immediacy, bringing a gritty, real-life vibrancy to proceedings. Publicity materials for the film emphasised the ability of the Open/Close Dundee street art project to 'reframe the familiar' in order to allow people to 'look at the city in a different way,' and certainly with the involvement of residents and artists alike, the director brings to life a heartfelt artistic effort to reinvigorate urban spaces and present surprising beauty even in the least expected of inner-city spaces.

Filmed entirely on location in Dundee, the film resembled its subject matter in the sense that it proved to be a burst of dazzling colour and infectious energy which helped to spotlight and enhance its surroundings. Gill includes interviews with the artists, provides time-lapse sequences where the artwork can be seen coming to life, and records the reactions of the public to these new creative visual works once they are on display. In so doing, *Open Close Movie* emphasises the transformative nature of art – from the boldest expressions to the most understated and hidden curiosities — to play an important part in urban regeneration and engage communities in creativity. The documentary premiered at the Dundee Contemporary Arts Centre in May 2018.

JUTE, JAM AND JIM McLEAN

YEAR: 1987
DIRECTOR: Ross Wilson
PRODUCTION COMPANY: Scottish Television

Jim McLean is a legendary sporting figure regarded with enormous respect in Dundee, and – perhaps fittingly – a documentary examining his impact on the city's footballing history, *Jute, Jam and Jim McLean*, has become one of the most instantly-recognisable of its type. McLean was the longest-serving manager of Dundee United, with a remarkable tenure spanning from 1971 to 1993, and to date has been the most successful in the club's history. He was the winner of the inaugural Scottish Football Writers' Association Manager of the Year Award in 1987, and his name was added to the Scottish Football Hall of Fame in 2025.

Broadcast on the 27th of February 1987 as part of STV's *Scottish Report* series, the documentary followed the McLean-led Dundee United as the team prepared for a titanic struggle in that year's UEFA quarter final match against Barcelona. The manager's legendary tenacity and strategic talent is highlighted, as was the economic depression facing the city of Dundee at the time. Unemployment had a deleterious effect on the club, with Tannadice Park hosting around 6,000 to 7,000 spectators per match – even in spite of the team's continued success at the time – simply due to fans being too cash-strapped to afford tickets. Ross Wilson's feature presents a fascinating glimpse into the city during the 1980s, and emphasises McLean's astonishing capacity to drive on his players to sporting success. The feature provides a unique cultural artefact which explores much more than football – the spirit of Dundee and its people at a pivotal period in the city's history is very much in the filmmaker's spotlight.

In his time as manager, McLean oversaw Dundee United win the Scottish League Cup in 1979 and 1980, and a Scottish Football League title in 1982/83, along with reaching domestic cup finals on another eight occasions. Awarded an honorary Doctor of Law degree by the University of Dundee in 2011, his professional achievements as a football manager will long be remembered, and he spurred his team on to dizzying heights during the course of his career. Though he died in 2020, McLean's lasting legacy has been honoured by a bronze memorial statue sculpted by Alan Heriot which is situated at Tannadice Park.

GREAT BRITISH RAILWAY JOURNEYS

YEAR: 2024
DIRECTOR: Cassie Farrell
PRODUCTION COMPANY: Talkback Thames/Boundless/Naked

Since 2010, former Westminster cabinet minister Michael Portillo has been entertaining audiences by retracing some of Britain's most noteworthy and historically significant train excursions as part of the documentary series *Great British Railway Journeys*. With 290 episodes produced at time of writing, over a total of sixteen series to date, this perennially popular staple of TV shows no sign of slowing down.

Airing on the 29th of March 2024 as part of the series' fifteenth season, 'Dundee to Loch of the Lowes' saw Portillo continue with his well-established format of following a particular journey on the British railway network and explaining its cultural or historical importance. This particular trip saw him crossing the Tay Rail Bridge to disembark in Dundee, where he visits the McManus Museum and Art Gallery and discovers the work of famed photographer Joseph McKenzie (often considered 'the father of modern Scottish photography').

Portillo's exploration of McKenzie's work takes him to Duncan of Jordanstone College of Art and Design (part of the University of Dundee, and regarded as one of Britain's finest schools of art and design) where he meets accomplished artist Calum Colvin – a one-time student of McKenzie's work – who speaks candidly about the art of photography before giving the presenter some instruction in the delicate skill of handling and developing film negatives. The rest of the episode sees Portillo visiting the city of Perth to view the noteworthy Victorian era Wellshill Cemetery on Feus Road, as well as conversing with folk singer-songwriter Fraser Bruce, before concluding his journey at Dunkeld and Birnam where he stops at the beautiful Loch of the Lowes to see ospreys in their natural habitat.

This informative Dundee adventure marked the conclusion of a five episode Scottish railway journey for Portillo that year, which also included Loch Lomond to Kelvinbridge, Glasgow to Cumbernauld, Shawlands to Livingston, and Edinburgh to Queensferry.

A SHOT AT GLORY

YEAR: 2000
DIRECTOR: Michael Corrente
PRODUCTION COMPANY: Butcher's Run Films/Eagle Beach Productions

Creating a fascinating crossover between Hollywood glamour and Scotland's favourite sporting pastime, football, *A Shot at Glory* saw multi-award-winning American actor Robert Duvall taking on the role of the manager of fictional Second Division Scottish Football League club Kilnockie FC as they fight to overcome many trials and problems in an attempt to reach the Scottish Cup Final. Providing further star power was an array of established performing talent including Michael Keaton, Brian Cox, Cole Hauser, and prominent Scottish footballer and manager Ally McCoist.

Gordon McLeod (Duvall), a veteran manager of a football team based in a proud fishing town, finds himself faced with an existential crisis when American owner Peter Cameron (Keaton) decides that he wants to relocate the club to the Irish city of Dublin. Further complicating matters is McLeod's tempestuous relationship with his son-in-law Jackie McQuillan (McCoist), a talented footballer nudging middle age who has recently been transferred from Arsenal and whose behaviour is becoming increasingly problematic. Can the two strong-willed men temporarily disregard their differences in order to turn around the club's fortunes, or is Kilnockie doomed to lose its team?

While the feature was primarily filmed in the Fife town of Crail – which doubled as the fictional settlement of Kilnockie – a number of additional scenes were shot in Arbroath, Angus. Duvall's character, Gordon McLeod, is thought to be based in part on Raith Rovers manager John McVeigh, and the actor spent considerable time researching that team's performance – including attending numerous matches – while several former Raith Rovers players appeared in the film, such as Peter Heatherstone, Didier Agathe, and Andy Smith. (Raith Rovers had unexpectedly beaten Celtic to the League Cup in 1994 – a sporting achievement which was an obvious influence for *A Shot at Glory*.) The film also contained the breakthrough role of famed Glasgow-based film, TV, and theatre actor Kirsty Mitchell, who played McLeod's daughter, Kate.

UNDER THE SKIN

YEAR: 2013
DIRECTOR: Jonathan Glazer
PRODUCTION COMPANY: Film4/British Film Institute/Silver Reel/Creative Scotland/Sigma Films/FilmNation Entertainment/Nick Wechsler Productions/J.W. Films/Scottish Screen/UK Film Council

Hollywood superstar Scarlett Johansson may have seemed like an incongruous choice for a film about an alien being who stalks the length and breadth of Scotland seeking lone men to prey on. And yet, this complex and far-reaching science fiction feature made excellent use of her famed acting skills; Johansson creates an inscrutable character who proves to be as enigmatic as she is deadly. Based loosely on Michel Faber's novel from 2000, the film marked the culmination of a long creative gestational period for director Jonathan Glazer, who had developed the concept for over a decade before it finally reached the big screen.

The story concerns an unnamed woman (Johansson) who travels from urban to rural locales and back as she lures unsuspecting men into a trap. Expecting an entirely different kind of 'close encounter,' they are each incarcerated and subjected to an unfathomable chemical process. However, while predatory, she seems genuinely bewildered by the appearance and functions of her body. Eventually, after many confrontations (most of them surreal), she is violently attacked by a sadistic logger (Dave Acton) in the wilderness, and her true form is revealed – the woman is actually an extraterrestrial being (Jessica Mance). Alarmed, the logger burns her alive, bringing her earthly incursion to an end.

Much of *Under the Skin*'s inexplicable events are left to the viewer to interpret; even the characters are rarely named (and are instead given impersonal monikers such as 'the Nervous Man,' 'the Pick-Up Man,' and so on), while the protagonist's true intentions are left wide open to individual analysis, winning screenwriters Glazer and Walter Campbell both critical praise and industry plaudits. Special effects were used sparingly, and great care is taken to present the often-disorienting action from the alien woman's perplexing perspective. Filming took place all over Scotland, with location filming in locations including Buchanan Street and Argyle Street in Glasgow, Tantallon Castle in North Berwick, Almondvale in Livingston, Wishaw, Port Glasgow, Kilsyth, North Berwick, Wanlockhead, Lochgoilhead, and – of most interest to this book – Auchmithie Beach, near Arbroath.

MOONACRE

YEAR: 1994
DIRECTOR: Robin Crichton
PRODUCTION COMPANY: Edinburgh Film and Video Productions

The wild beauty of Auchmithie Beach was rarely depicted quite as memorably than it was in 1994's *Moonacre*, a six-part TV adaptation of Elizabeth Goudge's 1946 children's novel *The Little White Horse*. Airing between 6th April and 11th May 1994, the miniseries featured a screenplay by William Corlett, and supporting parts for many well-known actors including Noah Huntley, Iain Cuthbertson, and Miriam Margolyes.

When her father dies in 19th century England, young orphan Maria Merryweather (Camilla Power) is sent to live at the enigmatic Moonacre Manor in the countryside. Aided by her devoted governess, Miss Heliotrope (Jean Anderson), and her beloved spaniel Wiggins, Maria soon strikes up a rapport with her new guardian (and cousin) Sir Benjamin Merryweather (Philip Madoc). Not all is quite as it seems at Moonacre, however, and Maria soon finds herself accompanied by a bewildering variety of enchanted animals as she gradually uncovers a puzzling secret that dates back right to the very genesis of the estate.

Much of the action of *Moonacre* was filmed in Slovenia, including the imposing Predjama Castle – a remarkable Renaissance building constructed around a 123 metre-high cliff face, which doubles for the fictional Moonacre mansion. However, scenes were also shot on location at Auchmithie, with a crew arriving in the village in the July of 1993 to film in the area – including in atmospheric caves along the beach. While the landscape proves suitably striking, the location did of course pose a perennial challenge for production crews when filming near the sea – taking note of tidal times was crucial in order to avoid being cut off by encroaching water.

The Little White Horse was later adapted for cinema, albeit more loosely, as *The Secret of Moonacre* in 2008. Directed by Gábor Csupó and starring Dakota Blue Richards as Maria, the film – like its TV forebear – featured a who's who of acting talent including Tim Curry, Natascha McElhone, Ioan Griffudd, and Juliet Stevenson. Unlike the earlier *Moonacre*, however, the movie featured extensive location filming throughout Hungary as well as in London – but not in Scotland.

RAT ON A HIGHWAY

YEAR: 2021
DIRECTOR: Vivek Singh Chauhan
PRODUCTION COMPANY: Roth Productions/The Production Headquarters/TPHQ

Rat on a Highway was a Bollywood production which has followed the example of an increasing number of India-produced motion pictures in recent years – it was filmed not in Asia, but rather on location in Scotland. Directed by Vivek Chauhan, the movie's screenplay was by Jagdish Metla and drew upon extensive filming throughout the East Coast during 2019.

The film featured the plight of the mysteriously-named M.T. (Randeep Hooda), an advertising executive who is unable to remember the past two days of his life. Strangely enough, this amnesia soon turns out to be among the least of his problems – his situation is more precarious than he may initially have expected, thanks to the aftermath of a car crash, and unravelling the conundrum behind his missing memories might just prove to be more perilous than he had initially imagined.

With dialogue in both English and Hindi, *Rat on a Highway* was filmed in Dundee, Arbroath, and Brechin, and made full use of the many different terrains and environments offered by Tayside and Angus. The film's budget was modest; only three cameras were used across the entire production, with most of the scenes taking place at night to avoid any costly disruptions to the action. Principal photography with the actors was completed in less than a month.

Produced by Mohaan Nadaar, *Rat on a Highway* drew upon an international cast, with Hooda joined by actors including Selina Youngerman, Jithu Paul, Nisha Aaliya, Yasir Abbas, Ellie Flory Fawcett, and Amber Joseph. Metla's script contains plenty of twists to keep thriller enthusiasts engaged, and the range of characters was nothing if not versatile in its adaptability to the elaborate plot. The majestic Angus coastline even featured in the film's pre-publicity, with Hooda – complete with his character's cuts-and-bruises injury make-up having been applied to the actor's face – posting selfies to the Internet between scenes.

1300 SHOTS

YEAR: 2021
DIRECTOR: Mark Lyken
PRODUCTION COMPANY: Soft Error

A documentary with a difference, *1300 Shots* was a remarkable testament to the power of the creative arts. Mark Lyken's single-shot film, which lasts for an hour and a quarter, follows two long-term patrons of Dundee's The Steps arthouse cinema twenty years after its closure, to observe them watching one final film on the premises – each of them sitting in their own personal favourite seat in the auditorium.

The *1300 Shots* of the film refers to Sergei Eisenstein's masterpiece of Russian cinema, *Battleship Potemkin (1925)* – starring Aleksandr Antonov and Vladmir Barskiy – a silent historical film chronicling the Russian Revolution of 1905, which famously consisted of 1300 individual shots in total. The patrons, Laura Walker and Mike Kane, watch the action avidly… though not without the odd moment where they stop to take in the cinema around them, acknowledge each other, and underscore the human quality of engaging with a motion picture. But how much of their emotional reaction captured by this portrait film is motivated by the power of Eisenstein's cinema, and how much is due to their nostalgia for the building itself and all the films they had each previously watched there?

The camera is fixed on both patrons separately, and as such the feature was made available both as a standard (split-screen) film as well as an installation version (two channel) where the footage of each individual patron is screened synchronously. The result was a fascinating expression of what it means to be a spectator – consuming artistic content and reacting to it in real time. Lyken had himself been a patron of The Steps cinema in its heyday, prior to its closure in the 1990s, and had remembered Kane and Walker from his time there – hence their invitation to be involved. The location is now the equally-beloved The Steps theatre, situated within Dundee Central Library in the Wellgate Centre.

The production of *1300 Shots* was supported by the Department of Film Studies at the University of St Andrews, as well as Creative Scotland, Live Borders, Leisure and Culture Dundee, Dumfries and Galloway Council, Dundee Local History Centre, and LUX Scotland.

THE LIGHTHOUSE STEVENSONS

YEAR: 2011
DIRECTOR: Les Wilson
PRODUCTION COMPANY: Caledonia Sterne and Wyld

A documentary which follows the remarkable achievements of the Stevenson family, *The Lighthouse Stevensons* explores the efforts of these far-seeing engineers in providing some much-needed safety along the Scottish coastline with the establishment of a series of lighthouses. Their first, and arguably most iconic, lighthouse was the Bell Rock, which is located just off the coast of Arbroath.

First broadcast on BBC2 Scotland on 1st February 2011, the programme outlines the dynasty of Stevenson engineers who were responsible for planning and then constructing more than eighty lighthouses during the nineteenth and twentieth centuries. Narrated by actor Denis Lawson, the documentary had been timed for release exactly two hundred years after the Bell Rock Lighthouse had been built in 1811. The positive impact of these buildings on maritime safety has proven to be incalculable.

Starting with civil engineer Robert Stevenson (grandfather of the famed novelist Robert Louis Stevenson), designer of the Bell Rock Lighthouse, *The Lighthouse Stevensons* discusses the immense logistical difficulties that had to be overcome in building these towering structures in some of the most perilous locations on the coastline, battling both tidal concerns and engineering complications. Stevenson would go on to design many other lighthouses in his lifetime, including at the Isle of May, Buchan Ness, Cape Wrath, and Dunnet Head, saving countless lives from navigation accidents as a result.

Robert Stevenson was, of course, only the first of his family to be involved in the construction of lighthouses, and the documentary follows other, later members – from Thomas Stevenson to David Alan Stevenson – who would also leave their mark on this difficult yet essential enterprise. Today, the Bell Rock Lighthouse remains the world's oldest working sea-washed lighthouse, and is a perennially popular tourist sight for visitors to Arbroath. (The lighthouse itself has been automated since October 1988, and is now remotely monitored from Edinburgh.)

IT'S MY CITY!: DUNDEE, BRITAIN'S BIGGEST VILLAGE

YEAR: 1989
DIRECTOR: John Chesworth Wigger
PRODUCTION COMPANY: BBC North West

It's My City! was a travelogue series which ran for nine episodes between 1988 and 1989. It featured a plethora of celebrities such as Eamonn Holmes, Glenda Jackson, Bill Paterson, and Kate Adie as they visited towns of cultural and historical significance around the British Isles. These locations were chosen as a result of a competition to find some of the most inspirational and far-reaching community projects in the country, leading the production team to a wide variety of urban destinations such as Belfast, Liverpool, Sunderland, and Glasgow.

Presented by Joanna Lumley, one episode of the series – broadcast on the 20th of June 1989 – centred on Dundee, and drew on the many new and innovative community projects taking place in the city at that time. These included a visit to Radio Tay, which had been broadcasting since October 1980 and was then based at its famous headquarters in the city's North Isla Street. Serving Tayside and the north-east of Fife, the station became renowned not just for its array of top broadcasting talent – including Mark Goodier, Eddie Mair, and Dave Bussey – but also its innovative Campus Radio initiative which enabled the broadcasting of educational content in collaboration with colleges in the area.

Dundee, Britain's Biggest Village featured interviews with a variety of famous locals including playwright Gordon Burnside, singer-songwriter Billy Mackenzie, and artist Bob McGilvray. Taken together, this painted a vibrant and inspirational picture of Dundee as a creative hotspot, showcasing just how valuable the artistic output of Dundonians was continuing to be even given the economic difficulties of the period.

More than anything, the series proved – just as it had with other cities around the country – that at the heart of all effective community initiatives is the collective effort of people working together towards a common goal. With Lumley as an engaging host, *Dundee, Britain's Biggest Village* is a fascinating snapshot of a city with no shortage of innovation and community focus, auguring well for its future.

A LIFE MORE ORDINARY

YEAR: 2002
DIRECTORS: Kimber Cox, Paul Dundee, and Anna Newell
PRODUCTION COMPANY: Dundee Repertory Theatre/Memphis Playhouse on the Square/Reptile46 Productions

A Life More Ordinary was a stage play which came about as a cultural exchange collaboration between Dundee Repertory Theatre and the Memphis Playhouse in Tennessee. Dundee Rep, as it has become known, was formed in 1939 and has been the home of world-leading acting talent ever since. Its many noteworthy alumni and players have included Richard Todd, Lynn Redgrave, Brian Cox, Hannah Gordon, Ian McDiarmid, Alan Cumming, and even Donald Sutherland.

The action of the film – which is a fantastical comedy — follows the events of the play, and focuses on the life of a Dundee youth, H.C. (Stephen Samson), who has a girlfriend based in Memphis named Dee (Louise Smyth). With a somewhat vivid imagination, H.C. begins to envisage his life as a series of film scenes, which play out – complete with some larger than life characters from history and cinema – as his story unfolds. These flamboyant figures include William Wallace (Sandy Jack), the Godfather (Reed Bouchillon), and the Sundance Kid (Darren Domm).

The conceit of having two protagonists separated by the Atlantic (with all of the cultural differences that this situation suggests) perfectly emphasised the ethos of this collaborative production, with the two companies – in Dundee and Memphis respectively – coming together seamlessly to tell the story of a deeply unconventional romance. H.C.'s somewhat tenuous grasp of reality is employed for comic effect, as well as for more general entertainment, and yet his flights of fancy also drive the narrative to a suitably offbeat conclusion.

Paul Dundee, one of the film's directors, would later helm *A Life More Ordinary: The Documentary* (2016), which interviewed many of the people involved in this highly ambitious 2002 transatlantic production and pieced together the significant technical challenges which had to be overcome in order to make it the success it became.

NO TIME (MUSIC VIDEO)

YEAR: 2021
DIRECTOR: Khaled Spiewak
PRODUCTION COMPANY: Fingerclick Productions/Strangeblud Film/SocialEyes

Dundee-based musician India Rose (an artist sometimes styled as 'IndiaRos3') made waves in 2021 when she released a music video to accompany the release of her new house dance track *No Time*. Having won a Scottish Alternative Music Award earlier that year, Rose was awarded funding from Creative Scotland to produce a music video for her latest song, and decided to set the action in the city of Dundee itself. One of the main attractions was the creative involvement of Annie Mitchell, who had been a member of the art department on the production of *Star Wars: The Rise of Skywalker* in 2019.

The action was very much intended to display an urban edge, and to showcase the contrast between the energetic and the mysterious within an inner-city environment. It follows a group of young women (including Rose herself) having a good time on a day out together… but not all is as it first appears, as they each don masks and speed off in a car. Soon, night has fallen in the city, and the trio chase down a secretive figure and knock him unconscious with a baseball bat. When he regains consciousness, he discovers that he has not been kidnapped by a street gang, but rather restrained by an old acquaintance. Yet rather than being a joke, as he supposes, the women make off with his bag of contraband – guaranteeing retribution against him from whoever he was trafficking it to. This sets him panicking as the light dies, leaving him tied to a chair in a nondescript warehouse.

Rose has explained in interviews that the theme of the film was female solidarity in the face of male infidelity, culminating in the empowerment that makes the video's motor-mouthed antagonist first fearful and then utterly hopeless in the face of his situation. With location filming around urban Dundee, and especially in the West End, the video was directed by Khaled Spiewak, who had previously been the editor of 2020's *Schemers* and also the screenwriter and director of short film *Happy Hour* in 2018. *No Time* also featured appearances by Natalie Bullions, Shania Evans, Ryan McAteer, and hip-hop artist Princyboii, as well as a voiceover from special guest Andy Bullick – the resident host at Dundee's famous Icebreaker comedy club – as a radio announcer 'DJ Damon.'

REMEMBER US (MUSIC VIDEO)

YEAR: 2019
DIRECTORS: Tamara Searle and Rhian Hinkley
PRODUCTION COMPANY: National Theatre of Scotland

Remember Us was the first music single to be produced by the National Theatre of Scotland. It was performed by Kayleigh Shields, who at the time was a student at Dundee and Angus College, and was written by Shields and Harry Myers Covill. The song came about on account of *Futureproof*, a project initiated by the National Theatre the year beforehand, with the intention of encouraging new creative talent as part of Scotland's Year of Young People in 2018. Australia's Back to Back Theatre, which had worked on a film-making project with Dundee's youth, was invited to collaborate on a performance project entitled *Radial*, from which *Remember Us* was eventually born.

The video features Shields performing her song, accompanied by many supporting performers, as a variety of environments appear around them – from the urban to the rural. *Remember Us* was filmed between the 5th and 9th of June 2018 at a variety of locations in and around Dundee, including City Square, beneath the Tay Bridge, Tentamuir Forest, Broughty Ferry, the Greenmarket Car Park, and West Ward Works. In the course of just a few minutes, the video illuminates the wide variety of surroundings which can be found within Dundee and its surrounding area, revealed here as a backdrop to a celebration of movement and awareness.

Remember Us certainly succeeded in its primary purpose of showcasing emerging artistic talent amongst Scotland's youth (not least as Shields was only seventeen years old at the time the video was produced), but it was also an excellent example of what can be made possible when organisations come together to produce something truly original and inventive. The video credited many local societies, companies, and associations who took part in its production, including D.C. Thomson, Dundee City Council, the Forestry Commission Scotland, Dundee Repertory Theatre, Scottish National Heritage, TayScreen, Dundee Dance Studio, the Scottish Dance Theatre, and a plethora of others, emphasising the city's commitment to the arts not just in the present, but also for its future.

CALIFORNIA SCHEMIN'

YEAR: 2025
DIRECTOR: James McAvoy
PRODUCTION COMPANY: Homefront Productions/Blazing Griffin/Patriot Pictures/Tartan Bridge Films

With countless international big budget productions to his name, James McAvoy has become one of Scotland's most storied acting talents of recent decades, having been active on stage and the big screen since the mid-1990s. An award-winner of multiple industry plaudits, there has been great anticipation surrounding his possible move into film directing, and in 2025 he would make his long-awaited debut behind the camera with *California Schemin'*.

Based upon the exploits of rap singers Silibil 'n' Brains – thought to be Californians, but actually the pairing of Dundonian musicians Gavin Bain and Billy Boyd – the film was based on Bain's autobiographical work *Straight Outta Scotland* (2010). It elaborates on the astonishing real-life story of how Bain (Séamus McLean Ross) and Boyd (Samuel Bottomley) affected American accents in order to win the attention of the music industry at the turn of the millennium. Unable to secure management when using their natural Scottish accents, they quickly secured representation as soon as they began masquerading as Californians, and eventually signed a record deal with Sony Music UK, appeared on MTV, and at one point toured live with Eminem. McAvoy also appears in the film, in the role of Neotone Records executive Anthony Reid.

California Schemin' premiered on 6th September 2025 at the Toronto International Film Festival, and featured extensive filming in both Dundee and Glasgow. In Dundee, shooting took place at the imposing Dudhope Court tower block near Lochee Road, as well as throughout the Hilltown area of the city including Dudhope Street. Some scenes also took place outside Tannadice Park, home to Dundee United Football Club. The Glasgow filming included some well-known areas of the city including Glasgow Green, the Barrowlands area, Queen Street Railway Station, Maryhill Park Circus, and Renfield Lane. Given McAvoy's own Glaswegian roots, it seemed only fitting that the film should retain such affection for the Dear Green Place as it so obviously does for the City of Discovery.

THE HIDDEN PERSUADERS

YEAR: 2011
DIRECTOR: Wayne Dudley
PRODUCTION COMPANY: Dudley Dangerous Productions

A micro-budget production filmed entirely in Dundee, *The Hidden Persuaders* has become something of a cult classic. With no connection to Vance Packard's famous 1957 book of the same name, the film – which was written and directed by Wayne Dudley – makes use of a fascinating premise and a hard-working cast of talented actors to tell an intriguing tale of manipulation and subliminal messaging.

The story revolves around the death of a rock singer – the lead vocalist of fictional band Processed Minds – who appears to have met their demise accidentally as a result of being under the influence of drugs. But investigative reporter Frank Cash (Dayle Teegarden) isn't so sure. His suspicions are raised by a number of unexpected circumstances which gradually emerge surrounding the singer's death, even though the police believe there is no case to investigate, and soon he finds himself knee-deep in a far-reaching conspiracy – one which suggests a web of corruption so comprehensive, Cash himself might just be the next in line to be murdered.

The Hidden Persuaders marked Dudley's debut as a film director, and toys with the issue of psychological manipulation – asking pointed questions about the forces that silently convince us about how we should live our lives, what our preferences should be, and how we should commit our personal resources. It won the film not just critical praise, but also a solid reputation amongst independent movie buffs. With Dudley's thoughtful screenplay and performances from actors including Stephen Samson, Rez Kempton, Tim Seyfert, Nicky Modlin, and Siobhan Callas, the film packs a considerably greater punch than its modest budget might at first suggest.

Winner of Best Experimental Film at the New York Big Mini-DV Festival in 2011, *The Hidden Persuaders* was filmed in and around Dundee, making great use of the city's architecture to conjure up a moody urban atmosphere. It may not be the best-known feature ever to be shot in the area, but it's certainly one that is worth seeking out.

DOG DAYS

YEAR: 2023
DIRECTOR: James Price
PRODUCTION COMPANY: Channel X Hopscotch

A thoroughly contemporary miniseries which dealt with heavyweight issues such as the cost of living crisis, substance addiction, and homelessness, *Dog Days* was filmed in Dundee throughout the summer of 2022 before being broadcast the following year. Directed by James Price, who also penned the screenplays, it was made available in a feature-length cut on BBC iPlayer as well as a serialised version.

Zoso (Connor McCarron) is living on the streets, and his life appears to be in a very bad place. A complex character, he struggles with violent impulses, and yet he also proves himself to be warm and empathetic at times. In particular, he longs to see his estranged daughter, and recognises that in order to do so he must try to improve his outlook for the future. New hope appears to blossom when music teacher Grace (Lois Chimimba) discovers that Zoso has hidden performance talents and encourages him to make the most of them. A stolen guitar and some unexpected good fortune sets him on his way, but can he ride the wave of deliverance all the way to liberation from his current circumstances?

Lauded for the strength and sincerity of its central performances, and the quality of its supporting players, *Dog Days* was widely commended for its imaginative use of Dundee as a backdrop for the action. Just as Zoso is a character of considerable contradictions, so too are we shown the city's urban landscape as a place of contrasts – from gritty sequences set amidst crumbling, once-grand buildings to a glimpse of a more hopeful future, with gleaming modern buildings pointing towards regeneration and reinvigoration, Dundee almost becomes as much of a character in the drama as its human cast proves to be.

Dog Days met with considerable critical praise at the time of its release, with Conor McCarron being awarded a Royal Television Society Scotland Award for Best Actor as well as being nominated for a BAFTA Scotland Award, while producers David Brown, Carolynne Sinclair Kidd, and James Price won Best Drama at the Royal Television Society Scotland Awards for Best Drama.

HATTER'S CASTLE

YEAR: 1942
DIRECTOR: Lance Comfort
PRODUCTION COMPANY: Grafton Films

One of the more unusual films to feature Dundee was Lance Comfort's wartime-shot drama *Hatter's Castle*, which – to date – is considered the only motion picture to feature the 1879 Tay Bridge disaster on the big screen. Based on A.J. Cronin's 1931 novel of the same name, the film starred Robert Newton, Deborah Kerr, and James Mason, and had a budget estimated at around £80,000. It surprised many critics at the time of its release by becoming one of the most popular films of the year.

A Victorian-era melodrama set in the 1870s, the film features the life of James Brodie (Robert Newton), a successful milliner who serves a Clydeside community. His business success does little to conceal the fact that he is hard-hearted in his commercial dealings, but his family life is similarly cold-blooded. Lording it over his nearest and dearest, he is unaware that his daughter Mary (Deborah Kerr) is embroiled in a love affair with Irishman Dennis Foyle (Emlyn Williams). When this comes to light, Brodie takes it badly and violently disowns his daughter. Dennis, who had planned to marry her, is killed due to the Tay Bridge collapsing as the train he was travelling on crosses it. Due to Brodie's brutally dictatorial manner and endless emotional cruelty, his company fails and his family gradually falls apart. Ultimately only Mary has anything close to a happy ending when – in spite of the tragedy that has dogged her life – she elopes with the local doctor, Renwick (James Mason), in the hope of a better future.

Hatter's Castle was released in February 1942, though – due to its wartime release date – it wasn't to reach American audiences until April 1948. It was filmed at Denham Studios in Buckinghamshire, but its Tay Bridge sequence is the one that is generally regarded as its most striking – a quality that has persisted on account of the fact that no later film has since attempted to recreate the events of the disaster. Star Robert Newton was widely praised by reviewers for his restrained performance as the ruthless social climber who is so singularly obsessed with gaining power and position that he ultimately loses everything.

SHOPPING (MUSIC VIDEO)

YEAR: 2024
DIRECTOR: Harvey Payne and Elliot Hall
PRODUCTION COMPANY: The Boom Boom Palace

Welly, the indie pop band from Southampton, have been entertaining their fans since 2021, and have played Glastonbury as well as many other venues around the country. Never afraid to innovate, they received critical attention for their 2023 live album *Welly: Live in a Village Hall*, which was recorded on location (as the title suggests) in an empty village hall. Though based in Southampton, the band has travelled widely, and for their 2024 single *Shopping* they decided on Dundee's centrally-located Keiller Centre as the venue for their accompanying music video.

Located on the city's Chapel Street, the Keiller Centre was opened in 1979 and quickly established itself as a popular location for Dundonian shoppers. It took its name from the famous Keiller family, the world-famous marmalade manufacturers who helped to make Dundee synonymous with the distinctive preserve. It received considerable consumer footfall in the 1980s and '90s, but its fortunes changed from the 2000s onwards, with national retailers relocating and empty units multiplying. However, it remains affectionately regarded by many locals.

The video involves the band opening up a seemingly-disused unit in the centre, in which they find all of their instruments prepared and ready for the song. Surrounded by stock clearance items and shop closure signs, they perform the track while exploring the mostly-closed centre. As they take part in a dance number in the deserted mall, their retail-themed lyrics somehow help to emphasise the centre's faded glory, harking back to its days as a must-visit commercial destination. When the song ends, they leave their instruments and vacate the shop, returning it to its unoccupied state.

Shopping reached number 7 in the UK singles charts, and the music video was praised for its inventiveness while the track itself was favourably compared to the work of bands as diverse as Blur, Talking Heads, Kaiser Chiefs, and Franz Ferdinand. It has been proposed that the Keiller Centre may eventually be redeveloped into the Keiller Quarter, a mixed-use space which is intended to increase numbers, and attract tourists and students alike.

WATERPROOF

YEAR: 2018
DIRECTOR: Joel Hewett
PRODUCTION COMPANY: Fingerclick Productions

Directed and written by Joel Hewett, who is also its star, *Waterproof* was a comedy with thoroughly contemporary concerns about relationships, responsibilities, and the course of life in general. The film was set in Dundee, and made excellent use of residential and commercial locations around the city – including well-known sites and landmarks. In an interesting development for its year of production, it was filmed entirely in black and white, and on an estimated budget of just £1,500.

The action of *Waterproof* is based around the life of Jack (Hewett), a young Dundonian who longs for direction. Tired of freewheeling from week to week, and smarting after the end of a long-term relationship, he decides that the time has come for duty and dependability. But corralling his day-to-day existence into more organised regularity turns out to be more of an uphill struggle than he had initially realised, leading him into a series of unexpected digressions along the way. Thankfully Jack has friends Richey (Lewis Skelly) and Sarah (Lauren Dunlop) alongside to help him focus on his new-found sense of responsibility rather than slide into bad habits. But will any of them actually succeed?

Hewett is a Dundee-based film-maker, and as such he employs locations around the city with great care and obvious affection. There are pubs, apartments, and recognisable areas on display – not that the camera lingers too long on the obvious tourist hotspots, but rather prefers to explore local places of interest that many Dundonians are likely to know well. Like many *auteur*-led features, ranging from the work of Eric Rohmer to Richard Linklater, there is great emphasis placed on the interaction between characters; the conversation seems suitably spontaneous, with improvised sections of dialogue adding to proceedings rather than deviating too far from the narrative. Hewett takes care to build up a distinctively Scottish sense of community spirit, and if the film celebrates anything, it's the vitally important comfort of having people to look out for you at all stages of your life. *Waterproof* was screened at the Dundee Contemporary Arts Centre in the spring of 2019.

THE HOUSE WAS NOT HUNGRY THEN

YEAR: 2025
DIRECTOR: Harry Aspinwall
PRODUCTION COMPANY: Fingerclick Productions

A ghost story with a difference, *The House Was Not Hungry Then* was filmed at a property in Arbroath by writer/director Harry Aspinwall and featured performances by a range of Scottish talent including Bobby Rainsbury, Clive Russell, and Bill Paterson. The film subverts expectation by presenting an entirely fresh aspect on the haunted house mystery; rather than relying on conventional horror tropes, it toys with the audience's anticipation to create a genuinely tense viewing experience.

An unnamed young woman (Rainsbury), who is in search of her missing father (Paterson), breaks into a seemingly-innocuous house deep in the Scottish countryside. Believing that her estranged parent is resident there, she is disappointed to discover no trace of him. However, she soon learns – to her confusion and growing horror – that every visitor to the building is fated to disappear. She begins to understand that an entity is present in the house (or, indeed, may be the house itself), which is what has been causing the unsuspecting callers to vanish. But if this didn't present peril enough, the woman discovers that the property's assumed owner (Russell) has taken up the persona of a smarmy estate agent, and is actively luring in unwitting viewers in the knowledge that they will be consumed by the malign entity. Can the woman overcome this evil presence in time to make her escape, or is she doomed to follow the apparent fate of her father?

The House Was Not Hungry Then was released on the 22nd of March 2025, and won favourable comparisons with other similarly-themed experimental features such as Robert Zemeckis' *Here* (2024) and Steven Soderbergh's *Presence* (2024). With its static cinematography, distant perspectives, disconcerting soundscape, and absolute refusal to offer any easy answers about the events that unfold, the film was certainly something of an acquired taste, and it has divided horror fans in particular. Yet with its impressively low-key performances and well-judged set design, there is an undeniably tangible sense of nerve-wracking atmosphere and diffuse, non-specific threat which continues to grow as the film progresses. Aspinwall's feature was an official selection for the Cinequest Film Festival 2025.

FRANKENSTEIN

YEAR: 2025
DIRECTOR: Guillermo del Toro
PRODUCTION COMPANY: Bluegrass Films/Demilo Films/Double Dare You

At time of writing, the most recent film to feature Angus as a filming location is Mexican director Guillermo del Toro's highly-anticipated adaptation of Mary Shelley's seminal 1818 novel *Frankenstein*, which received its premiere in Venice on the 30th August 2025 (where it was nominated for the Golden Lion Award for Best Film) and is due for release in selected cinemas from 17th October, before being set to arrive on Netflix on the 7th November.

A truly epic rendering of Shelley's massively influential Gothic science fiction tale, del Toro's *Frankenstein* was made on a budget of $120 million and features Oscar Isaac as Victor Frankenstein, Jacob Elordi as the Creature, and a supporting cast full of international performance talent including Mia Goth, Lars Mikkelsen, Charles Dance, and Christoph Waltz. While the story of Dr Frankenstein's tragic hubris has become well-known the world over, del Toro had spoken of engaging with the project since 2007 and was determined to bring a fresh visual take to the tale whilst honouring the legacy of earlier cinematic adaptations such as the Universal horror movie of 1931, the Hammer Films version (and spin-offs) of 1957–74, and Kenneth Branagh's faithful big screen rendering of 1994.

As might be expected from such a big budget production, a variety of international locations were chosen for filming which included Cinespace Studios in Toronto; the University of Toronto; Markham, North Bay and North York in Ontario; Wilton House in Wiltshire; Burghley House in Lincolnshire; and Shepperton Studios in Surrey. However, location shooting took place in numerous Scottish towns and cities too, such as Glencoe; Dunecht House in Aberdeenshire; Glasgow Cathedral; Wardrop's Court, the Canongate, Lady Stair's Close, Parliament Square, Bakehouse Close, and Makars' Court in Edinburgh; and – most relevant to this book – Arbroath, including at Hospitalfield House, an historic manor (and now residential arts centre) which is believed to be the first art college in Britain. The inclusion of this imposing but much-loved building is testament to Angus's ongoing relevance as a filming location to productions of all origins and scales, from local independent features to huge global blockbusters.

Conclusion

Our journey through Dundee, Tayside, and Angus film locations reveals not only a fascinating past but also a dynamic future. The cobbled closes, sweeping coastlines, rugged glens, and striking cityscapes have long lent themselves to storytelling, quietly supporting productions both local and international. Yet what emerges most clearly is that this region is not simply a backdrop – it is a character in its own right, alive with atmosphere, history, and creative possibility.

Looking forward, there is every reason to believe that the screen presence of the area will continue to expand. Abertay University's CoSTAR Realtime Lab at Water's Edge in Dundee, with its cutting-edge virtual production capabilities, has already positioned the city as a pioneer in the future of filmmaking. Here, worlds can be built and reshaped in real time, offering a seamless blend of imagination and technology. This facility is not just an asset to the city but a beacon to the entire country, ensuring that Scotland remains at the forefront of artistic and technological innovation.

Part of the UK-wide CoSTAR (Convergent Screen Technologies and performance in Realtime) initiative, the lab is designed to bring together expertise in gaming, virtual production, visual effects, and performance capture. By leveraging Abertay University's long-established strengths in computer games education and research, the lab acts as a testbed for developing new methods of content creation, where digital and physical worlds can be blended seamlessly. This makes it possible for filmmakers and creatives to experiment with highly immersive, interactive techniques that are transforming the way stories are told on screen.

For Dundee and the surrounding region, the CoSTAR Realtime Lab represents a significant step forward in securing a place at the forefront of the future of film-making. The facility not only provides local and international productions with access to state-of-the-art virtual production tools, but it also fosters collaboration between academia, industry, and the arts. This creates unparalleled opportunities for new partnerships, skills development, and innovation-driven economic growth. In practical terms, it means filmmakers working in Tayside will be able to test and refine creative ideas in an environment that matches the technological sophistication of global studios, while also drawing on the region's distinctive landscapes and unique talent pool. As such, the lab is both a catalyst for local film production and a beacon of Dundee's growing role as a hub for next generation screen technologies.

But beyond the studio walls, the natural and cultural assets of Tayside and Angus remain compelling. The dramatic cliffs of Arbroath, the timeless riverside views of Broughty Ferry, the brooding majesty of Glamis Castle, and the urban vibrancy of Dundee's waterfront each offer settings that can rival any international destination. Crucially, the compact geography of the region allows filmmakers to move from medieval grandeur to modern chic, or from sweeping wilderness to bustling streets, within a single day's travel. Few parts of the world can offer such variety in so concentrated a space.

For visitors, this means not only the chance to walk in the footsteps of favourite films but to immerse themselves in the living, breathing culture that nurtures them. To visit Dundee, Tayside, and Angus is to discover a land where tradition and innovation sit side by side; where you might admire centuries-old architecture in the morning and step into a world-class digital production hub in the afternoon.

The story of film in this wonderful corner of Scotland is therefore not just about what has been shot here, but what could still be. The region is poised to welcome more productions, inspire more creative minds, and invite more audiences to see it anew. Dundee, Tayside, and Angus are ready not only to support the telling of stories, but to shape the future of how stories are told.

The lights are already shining, and the cameras are increasingly turning their gaze this way. The stage is set. And as the city of Dundee and its neighbouring towns continue to innovate, explore, and open their arms to the world, there is no doubt that the best scenes are still to come.

Visit the Set

Locations in Dundee, Tayside and Angus

Visit Dundee

Visit Angus

Leisure & Culture Dundee

Angus Alive

Screen Scotland

TayScreen

CoSTAR Realtime Lab

Dundee Heritage Trust

Dundee University

Abertay University

The McManus: Dundee's Museum and Art Gallery

V&A Dundee

The Verdant Works

RRS *Discovery*

Dundee Airport

Groucho's, Dundee

Caird Hall, Dundee

Dundee Law

Carnoustie Golf Links

Glamis Castle

Arbroath Abbey

Bell Rock Lighthouse

Photo Credits

Front Cover:	Image is Copyright © Jacob Boomsma at Shutterstock, all rights reserved.
Frontispiece:	Image by Gino Crescoli from Pixabay. Licensed under the Pixabay Licence.
Map:	Map of Dundee and the County of Angus by Nilfanion at Wikimedia Commons, and is licensed under the Creative Commons Attribution-Share Alike 3.0 Unported license. <*https://creativecommons.org/licenses/by-sa/3.0/*> Contains Ordnance Survey data © Crown Copyright and Database Right.
Panorama:	Image by Valentine Kulikov on Pexels. Licensed under the Pexels Licence.
Page iv:	Image from the authors' personal collection.
Page 3:	Image by PictureGuy20 on Wikimedia Commons and is licensed under the Creative Commons Attribution-Share Alike 4.0 International license. <*https://creativecommons.org/licenses/by-sa/4.0/*>
Page 6:	Image from the authors' personal collection.
Page 9:	Image by Tobias Patrick Wolf on Unsplash. Licensed under the Unsplash Licence.
Page 13:	Image by Saul Bandera Brotheridge on Pexels. Licensed under the Pexels Licence.
Page 14:	Image by mags1x from Pixabay. Licensed under the Pixabay Licence.

Page 18:	Image by Photo by Andy Fotheringham on Pexels. Licensed under the Pexels Licence.
Page 21:	Image is Copyright © Adrian T. Jones at Shutterstock, all rights reserved.
Page 25:	Image by NT Franklin from Pixabay. Licensed under the Pixabay Licence.
Page 26:	Image by Valentine Kulikov on Pexels. Licensed under the Pexels Licence.
Page 31:	Image is Copyright © Jarek Szaranek at Shutterstock, all rights reserved.
Page 32:	Image is Copyright © ZibiZ Photo at Shutterstock, all rights reserved.
Page 36:	Image by Valentine Kulikov on Pexels. Licensed under the Pexels Licence.
Page 39:	Image is Copyright © James McDowall at Shutterstock, all rights reserved.
Page 43:	Image is Copyright © JimMonkPhotography at Shutterstock, all rights reserved.
Page 44:	Image by Radu Daniel (MRD) on Pexels. Licensed under the Pexels Licence.
Page 48:	Image from the authors' personal collection.
Page 51:	Image from the authors' personal collection.
Page 55:	Image from the authors' personal collection.
Page 56:	Image from the authors' personal collection.
Page 60:	Image by Thomas Mills on Unsplash. Licensed under the Unsplash Licence.

Page 63:	Image by Tobias Patrick Wolf on Unsplash. Licensed under the Unsplash Licence.
Page 67:	Image by Ilya on Unsplash. Licensed under the Unsplash Licence.
Page 68:	Image is Copyright © Rob Atherton at Shutterstock, all rights reserved.
Page 72:	Image by David McCreight from Pixabay. Licensed under the Pixabay Licence.
Page 75:	Image by David McCreight from Pixabay. Licensed under the Pixabay Licence.
Page 79:	Image is Copyright © Mark Caunt at Shutterstock, all rights reserved.
Page 80:	Image by Zack Davidson on Unsplash. Licensed under the Unsplash Licence.
Page 84:	Image by Pete from Pixabay. Licensed under the Pixabay Licence.
Page 87:	Image by Seven-Of-Altea from Pixabay. Licensed under the Pixabay Licence.
Page 91:	Image by JoeSoap1952 from Pixabay. Licensed under the Pixabay Licence.
Page 92:	Image from the authors' personal collection.
Page 97:	Image is Copyright © iPlantsman at Shutterstock, all rights reserved.
Pages 98-99:	Image is Copyright © Jacob Boomsma at Shutterstock, all rights reserved.
Page 100:	Image is Copyright © The University of Abertay Dundee, all rights reserved, and is reproduced by kind permission of the copyright holder.

Page 103: Image is Copyright © The University of Abertay Dundee, all rights reserved, and is reproduced by kind permission of the copyright holder.

Page 104: Image is Copyright © AlanF at Shutterstock, all rights reserved.

Acknowledgements

We would like to thank the following people for their help and input into the research behind the writing of this book, which has been most thankfully appreciated:

- Paul Campbell of Leisure and Culture Dundee
- Dr Erin Farley of Dundee Local History Centre
- Iain E.F. Flett of Friends of Dundee City Archives
- Graeme Bletcher, Philip Vaughan, and Matthew Bett of Abertay University
- Katie Donnelly and Neil Paterson of Dundee Central Library
- Duncan Falconer of Lochee Library
- Barry Sullivan, Graeme Strachan, and Ross Crae of D.C. Thomson
- Eileen Budd, Storyteller and Folklorist
- Ingrid Thomson, Glamis Castle Archivist
- Julie Craik of TayScreen
- Robert Murray and Eleanor Jewson

About the Authors

Image © Julie Howden Photography

Dr Thomas Christie has many years of experience as a literary and publishing professional, working in collaboration with several companies including Cambridge Scholars Publishing, Crescent Moon Publishing and Applause Books. A passionate advocate of the written word and literary arts, over the years he has worked to develop original writing for respected organisations such as the Stirling Smith Art Gallery and Museum and a leading independent higher education research unit based at the University of Stirling. Additionally, he is regularly involved in public speaking events and has delivered guest lectures and presentations about his work at many locations around the United Kingdom.

Tom is a Fellow of the Royal Society of Arts and a member of the Society of Authors, the Federation of Writers Scotland and the Authors' Licensing and Collecting Society. He holds a first-class Honours degree in English Literature and a Master's degree in Humanities with British Cinema History from the Open University in Milton Keynes, and a Doctorate in Scottish Literature awarded by the University of Stirling. He is currently an Associate Lecturer with Forth Valley College's Stirling Campus, and since 2015 has served as Director of the award-winning Extremis Publishing Ltd.

Tom is the author of a number of books on the subject of modern film which include *Liv Tyler: Star in Ascendance* (2007), *The Cinema of Richard Linklater* (2008), *John Hughes and Eighties Cinema: Teenage Hopes and American Dreams* (2009), *Ferris Bueller's Day Off: Pocket Movie Guide* (2010), *The Christmas Movie Book* (2011), *The James Bond Movies of the 1980s* (2013), *Mel Brooks: Genius and Loving It!: Freedom and Liberation in the Cinema of Mel Brooks* (2015), *A Righteously Awesome Eighties Christmas: Festive Cinema of the 1980s* (2016), *The Golden Age of Christmas Movies: Festive Cinema of the 1940s and 50s* (2019), *John Hughes FAQ* (2019), *A Totally Bodacious Nineties Christmas: Festive Cinema of the 1990s* (2022), and *A Seriously Groovy Movie Christmas: Festive Cinema of the 1960s and 70s* (2024).

His other works include *Notional Identities: Ideology, Genre and National Identity in Popular Scottish Fiction Since the Seventies* (2013), *The Spectrum of Adventure: A Brief History of Interactive Fiction on the Sinclair ZX Spectrum* (2016), *Contested Mindscapes: Exploring Approaches to Dementia in Modern Popular Culture* (2018), *A Very Spectrum Christmas: Celebrating Seasonal Software on the Sinclair ZX Spectrum* (2021), and *Digital Pioneer Spirit: The Freewheeling Creative Innovation of Mel Croucher on the Home Microcomputer* (2025). He has also written a crowdfunded murder-mystery novel, *The Shadow in the Gallery* (2013), which is set during the nineteenth century in Stirling's historic Smith Art Gallery and Museum, and – in collaboration with archaeologist Dr Murray Cook – *Scotland's Christmas: Festive Celebrations, Traditions and Customs in Scotland from Samhain to Still Game* (2023).

Additionally, Tom has written two Scottish travel guides in partnership with his sister, Julie Christie, which are entitled *The Heart 200 Book: A Companion Guide to Scotland's Most Exciting Road Trip* (2020) and *Secrets and Mysteries of the Heart 200 Route* (2021).

For more information about Tom and his work, please visit his website at: **www.tomchristiebooks.co.uk**

Image © Laura Chalkley

Julie Christie has been working in different roles within business and the third sector for more than three decades. Over the years she has worked with a number of charitable organisations such as the Princess Royal Trust for Carers, the Aberlour Childcare Trust, the Alzheimer's Society, the Royal Voluntary Service and Town Break Dementia Care. She was also an associate with the University of Stirling, where she was involved in the development of Dementia Friendly Communities. Julie is currently the Communities and Fundraising Manager for Start Up Stirling, the city's food bank, providing a variety of services throughout the Stirling Council area for people experiencing financial hardship and food insecurity.

She brings considerable experience from the commercial retail industry, having held posts with famous national organisations including AstraZeneca, the NHS, Marks and Spencer, Goldsmiths, Thorntons and Laura Ashley. She holds a Bachelor of Nursing degree from the University of Glasgow and a Bachelor of Science degree with first-class Honours in Sociology and Social Policy from the Open University, which she loved doing as it concentrated on the things that fascinated her about people and culture as well as exploring how we can both see the same thing and yet hold an entirely different point of view.

Her hardest job was dealing with fraught brides when she worked in the wedding trade, where she had to develop her tea-making skills as well as occasionally mopping up tears! The most rewarding job of all – and also the worst-paid – was looking after her late Mum, who had to live with many chronic illnesses.

Julie had never tried being self-employed, so – given her passion for lifelong learning and literacy – the next logical step was to co-found a publishing business, Extremis Publishing Ltd., with her brother Tom. By roping him in to her grand plan, they were able to bring different life skills to the mix. The company specialises in arts, media and culture non-fiction, and their mission is to provide an eclectic range of interesting books, continuing in the long heritage of publishing in the city of Stirling. She is convinced that real life is always more interesting than fiction.

Julie has written two books in collaboration with her brother and co-director Tom Christie: *The Heart 200 Book: A Companion Guide to Scotland's Most Exciting Road Trip* (2020) and *Secrets and Mysteries of the Heart 200 Route* (2021). She also edits the regular *Extremis Etc.* newsletter, which is released every two months.

As Director of Extremis Publishing, in 2025 Julie was presented with the Publishing Businesswoman of the Year Award for Scotland at the Influential Businesswoman Awards.

Her view on life is that you should never be afraid to try new things, everyone should have a fair chance, that living life is way more interesting than doing the dusting, and that she has never found a box of chocolates that she hasn't liked yet!

For details of new and forthcoming books from Extremis Publishing, please visit our official website at:
www.extremispublishing.com

Follow us on social media at:

www.facebook.com/extremispublishing

www.linkedin.com/company/extremis-publishing-ltd-/

Subscribe to our regular newsletter at:

extremispublishing.substack.com

Hear our podcast on all good streaming audio providers

www.ingramcontent.com/pod-product-compliance
Lightning Source LLC
Chambersburg PA
CBHW061157010526
44119CB00059B/851